TEMPLE FOUNDATIONS

Essays on an Emerging Concept

By Richard A. Brown

Herald Publishing House
Independence, Missouri

Independence, Missouri
Printed in the United States of America

Library of Congress Cataloging-in-Publication Data
Brown, Richard A., 1951-
Temple foundations: essays on an emerging concept by Richard A. Brown.
p. cm.
ISBN 0-8309-0589-8
1. Temple (Independence, Mo. : Reorganized Church of Jesus Christ of Latter Day Saints) 2. Reorganized Church of Jesus Christ of Latter Day Saints—Doctrines. 3. Independence (Mo.)—Church history. 4. Reorganized Church of Jesus Christ of Latter Day Saints—Missions. I. Title.
BX8677.I53B76 1991 90-25794
246'.95'0977841—dc20 CIP

**For my children, Matthew and Bethany,
who someday may wonder
what life was like
before the Temple**

Table of Contents

Foreword

In Australia the story is told of a tribe of aboriginal people who for generations had camped on the banks of a great river. Flowing gracefully across the land, the river gave sustenance to all who camped on its shores. Over time, however, the river ceased to flow and its water became a billabong, a murky stagnant pool. When the intense heat of the Outback began to dry up the water, people were panic-stricken. How could fate be so unkind as to take away the only source of life? On the dry banks many of the aborigines sat, hoping for the river to flow again. A few more adventuresome souls thought to investigate the cause of the new situation. They went in search of why the water was disappearing, only to find that the river was not gone. It had simply changed its course upstream and was still flowing on to bless and nurture those who were prepared to open themselves to the new realities of life in the Outback.

Life, as everyone knows, is in constant flux. Modern society is experiencing change in all social and economic dimensions, and the rate of change is rapidly accelerating. No one can stop change; our best hope is to harness it and direct it toward useful and meaningful ends. Change has a positive edge to it, because with change come possibilities for new growth, new creativity, and new response to the multiple resources that life presents in such abundance.

Change in its many manifestations also faces the church today. With the building of the Temple in Independence, Missouri, the church is facing opportunities unprecedented in its history. Great expectations exist among the Saints that this Temple will in fact become a blessing to the church and through the church a blessing to the world. We do not know the full extent of this blessing. The shape and contours of the programs of ministry and outreach that shall emanate from the Temple are not yet operational or even clearly articulated in detail. But excitement for the new possibilities before us is running high.

The Temple shall be dedicated to the pursuit of peace. It will provide for the multiplicity of functions that were evident in Jesus' ministries, such as teaching, reconciliation, healing, servanthood activities, and leading people into the presence of God. Its programs of ministries shall be focused on strengthening the faith of all who enter its precincts, on leadership education, on preparation for witness, and on empowerment for Christian discipleship.

While it is not yet clear what all the possibilities for Temple ministries might be, the process of talking and listening together is a helpful way to explore options. Richard Brown has done much to encourage this process by the persuasive power of the written word. Constantly generating a rich supply of articles about the Temple, Richard is challenging us to offer our abundant gifts of intellect and insight to the development of our vision of the Temple.

This book is a collection of essays that calls us to think deeply and share broadly about how the Temple can affect the mission of the church in our times. In this book Richard holds before us multiple images for us to reflect on concerning how this edifice and the programs of ministries housed therein can impact the life of the world in a positive way.

Many who sit by the arid riverbanks of inadequate inherited notions concerning how God shall carry on the work of redemption in the world may find themselves challenged by the vision of this author. He gently encourages us to move forward in faith toward new commitments, new resolves, and new insights about the meaning of the Temple for today. He gives us new symbols and understandings to help us think together about how the Temple can interconnect with the congregations of the church to multiply the impact of the Saints in redemptive ministries that are so needed among the peoples of Earth.

Wayne Ham
Director of Temple Ministries

Introduction

I never intended to write a book on the Temple. It started as an essay here, an article there, a testimony somewhere else. Before long it led to more essays and articles, a contribution to a Temple School course, and an adult study guide to selected portions of the Doctrine and Covenants. It culminated in a master's thesis in the Park College Graduate School of Religion program.

Only now can I discern any kind of pattern in it all, and even there I'm not so sure it is anything more than an after-the-fact ordering or sorting, putting all the various parts into a manageable form. The church, too, is engaged in just that kind of sorting out right now regarding the Temple. It's a process that sometimes is called "stocking the kitchen."

When the new occupants of a house move in, they are faced with an almost monumental task of finding a place for everything. The kitchen, invariably, calls for the most choices to be made. On moving day a place is found and designated for the dishes and cutlery, the cereal boxes and soup cans, the wastebasket and the junk drawer. It's all brand-new, even though some choices are more or less determined by convenience or the location of appliances and traffic patterns.

Within a few days the newness begins to wear off and the occupants become comfortable with where everything goes. Shortly thereafter, those designated locations become where specific items *should* go. It's hard to say just when everything doesn't just *belong* in a particular place and when we feel it *ought* to go there, perhaps as some small part of the unfolding of the universe, but it always happens. The way we stock our kitchens on moving-in day is the way they stay until we move out or completely redecorate. Think about it. When was the last time you saw anyone empty all of their kitchen shelves and drawers just so they could put everything back in a different place? It has probably happened somewhere, to somebody, but I've never run across it.

In any event, whenever anyone asks me why I've written about the Temple, I tell them my kitchen story. The way we will stock and furnish the Temple (whether we're speaking of the building or the much greater and more important concept) is pretty much how it is going to be for a long, long time. Whether for lack of money, energy, personnel, or courage, we'll find a good reason or excuse *not* to go to the trouble to change things much. And so, let's do it right the first time.

The essays in this volume are not arranged chronologically, even though that might seem to be the most logical method. They begin with my most recent *Saints Herald* article on "Laying the Foundations" and hopscotch through the pages of *Restoration Witness* magazine, the *Herald*, *Restoration Studies IV*, and *Dialogue: A Journal of Mormon Thought*. That latter essay was probably the most challenging to write because I attempted to explain to a predominately Utah Mormon audience why we Reorganized Latter Day Saints are building this particular "Temple in Zion." It was difficult because our two religious communities share a history and a vocabulary, yet each interprets them in completely different ways.

Included as well are essays from the widely used Temple School course TL 100, The Temple, and three of the six chapters of *Studies in the Doctrine and Covenants, Volume 3* produced by the Christian Education Commission. They offer a mix of historical, social, and theological interpretations. Invariably there is some overlapping, but that merely highlights the fact that one cannot *do* theology without bumping up against historical study or social and cultural examination. The Temple has not arisen in a vacuum, after all.

One of my fantasies is to be a time traveler, zooming back and forth from the present moment. It's an exercise lived out in my mind rather than in some H. G. Wells-like contraption or a sleek, stainless steel DeLorean like the one in the movie, *Back to the Future*. I let my imagination respond to many questions:

What if the early Restoration church had built a temple in Independence instead of being driven out of Jackson County in 1833? What if Joseph Smith III's followers had moved back to the "Center Place of Zion" rather than Lamoni, Iowa, and erected the "House of the Lord" there in the late nineteenth century? What if Fred M. Smith's Saints had built a temple instead of an auditorium? What if we'd waited another generation before we broke ground for the Temple? How might our past, present, and future be different?

I've heard it said that we eventually will begin marking time in this church by "before Temple" and "after Temple." That's not as absurd, really, as it might seem. For the Temple is, I believe, the pivotal moment and event in all our history. Yet the building is really the least important part. I refer to it in one of these essays as a 300-foot-tall "tip of the iceberg," a visible sign of invisible grace. It can help us dream as we've never dared before:

Can we ever stop thinking of ourselves as "not Mormon" and start sharing and emphasizing the powerful, life-giving strengths of our movement instead? I believe we can.

Is it possible that this church can replace its patriarchal hierarchy with a prophetic and democratic community of believers empowered by the presence of an incarnate Christ within them? I believe it is.

Will we look honestly and critically at our past, at our triumphs and foibles, to accept that we are something other than heroes defending ourselves against the persecution of the outside world? I believe we can.

Have we the willingness to delve deeper into an understanding of "keeping the law" to see that it is not just paying tithing or making an annual financial accounting but being stewards of our relationship with the earth, our neighbors, and Divinity? I believe we can.

What gives me hope is the presence of the Temple in the literal and figurative center of our faith community. What a task, what a burden, what an opportunity, what a challenge.

The more I think and dream about the Temple, the less I realize I know and the riskier the whole enterprise seems. So maybe I should just stop dreaming and, instead, be content with the way things are. But I can't do that, because I keep hearing so many generations of Saints singing together, "We limit not the truth of God to our poor reach of mind. ...The Lord hath yet more light and truth. ... " Laying the foundations of the Temple includes "stocking the kitchen," and it's almost time to move in.

Richard A. Brown

Originally published in the ***Saints Herald*** *Vol. 137, No. 11 (November 1990): 13-16.*

1

Laying the Foundations

He was indignant and filled with sincere fury. But I listened anyway because I had known and respected him practically all my life.

Citing the words of the prophet Jeremiah to ancient Judah in the days before its destruction, he likened it to the current church situation: "How is it that we're supposedly building a Temple dedicated to peace, but what we've really had for almost thirty years is just cries of 'peace, peace.' But there is no peace; in fact, there's been anything but peace. Shouldn't that tell us something about the direction the leadership has been taking the church? I think Jeremiah had it right: 'Ask for the old paths, where is the good way, and walk therein, and ye shall find rest for your souls' " (Jeremiah 6:16).

The words of Jesus came to my mind: "Think not, that I am come to send peace on earth; I came not to send peace, but a sword" (Matthew 10:30). Jesus was talking about putting the priority of God's kingdom first. He finished with, "And he who taketh not his cross and followeth after me, is not worthy of me. He who seeketh to save his life shall lose it; and he who loseth his life for my sake shall find it" (Matthew 10:33-34).

In that sense I firmly believe the church for the sake of Christ has lost its life in order to find it. We have turned from proclaiming the One True Church to glorifying the One True God as we have entered many new parts of the world. This has not occurred as a result of careful planning and by implementing strategic evangelistic objectives but because God's Spirit has gone ahead, calling (and sometimes dragging) us forward.

The reason for this seemingly sudden transformation of the church has been a mystery. Was it just because the world has begun to change so rapidly, so dramatically? Perhaps only now can we look back and see what has really been happening. All that time we actually have been laying the foundations of Temple ministry.

Seen in that way, it becomes apparent that the Temple *building* is probably the least important element in the whole enterprise. That may seem to be an odd statement considering the cost and scope of the construction project, and it may not become apparent until some time after the building is dedicated and put in use. But that is within the nature of any ongoing, developing concept.

Yet the overarching purpose of the ministry of the Temple provides the greatest challenge right now. Long before the first surveyor's measurement, the first scoop of asphalt and dirt, or the first cubic yard of poured concrete, the Holy Spirit has been directing us in laying these spiritual foundations:

Heal the body, mind, and spirit

One of the first new areas to which the church was called was the Caribbean island nation of Haiti. There, in what perhaps should have been a tropical paradise, millions of Haitians comprised one of the poorest and most corrupt societies anywhere in the world. The immediate need was for health teams. As a result, dentists, physicians, and nurses traveled from the United States and Canada to set up dental and medical clinics.

Their work was valuable and appreciated, but it soon became obvious that it was, essentially, temporary and inadequate to meet the overwhelming needs of the native people. The lesson we learned was that filling dental cavities, bandaging wounds, or even ridding children of parasites would have little value without a long-term, wholistic approach to life-style and livelihood. The healing hands of Temple ministry must do far more than apply first aid; they must somehow seek transformation.

Today, in Haiti and elsewhere, the church continues to sponsor health clinics. But as part of that effort, we are training indigenous health-care workers, drilling wells for potable drinking water, and helping develop new livelihoods, jobs, and communities.

Establish worshiping communities

One of the most remarkable branches of the church is located in the southeast corner of the East African nation of Nigeria. The village of Ikot Oku Mfang is a special, sacred place. There is a large school and medical clinic as well as the Southeast Nigeria Church headquarters. But what is most remarkable is the spirit of this community lead by two amazing individuals—Grace and Sunday Charlie Akpan.

The hundreds of Saints in this village do not think of church, community, education, health care, and routine daily life in separate categories. In Ikot Oku Mfang one "worships" all the time; there is a constant connection and relationship with the Creator that finds joyful expression every day. This is evident in the African melodies and dance steps that are so much a part of the Sunday morning offering and in the planting, harvesting, cooking, and cleaning every other day of the week. The greatest testimony of these Saints is their community, which witnesses of God's love. They don't have to "go to church" to seek divine presence; they recognize their relationship with God at all times.

Some in the North American church have expressed concern that perhaps the Africans are baptizing too many, too soon, and that they should wait for sufficient money and trained ministers to become available. The twofold fear is that such missions will be a financial drain and a theological danger because of so many converts inexperienced in the ways of the church. Yet clearly, the Holy Spirit came to Ikot Oku Mfang long before the Reorganized Church got there. What would happen if we chose to not run to catch up?

Bear the burden of sins

In spring 1990 the church celebrated its twenty-fifth anniversary among the Sora tribespeople of India. Thousands of Saints and friends gathered in the second largest RLDS conference anywhere in the world. This was certainly a far cry from November 9, 1965, when Apostles Clifford Cole and Charles Neff, on their first trip to India, baptized Gurbux Singh Chawla and twenty-eight others in Orissa State, ordained Chawla an elder, and celebrated Communion for the first time.

Within a few years, however, the Soras presented the church with what became one of the most divisive issues in our history. Polygamy is a fairly common cultural practice there, and it wasn't long before polygamists requested baptism. The matter was passed up the administrative line and eventually exploded at the

1970 World Conference in Independence. The debate was loud and acrimonious.

Many delegates contended that the church *under no circumstances* should become stained by the one practice the Reorganization has fought so hard against for so long. They insisted that polygamists renounce the practice and dissolve their marriages before the church could admit them to its fellowship.

Others wondered what would happen to Sora women suddenly cut off from their polygamous marriages. Considering their restrictive culture, would they be better off dead? If so, shouldn't the church offer a more caring, Christlike response? It came two years later in this prophetic message:

> Monogamy is the basic principle on which Christian married life is built. Yet, as I have said before, there are also those who are not of this fold to whom the saving grace of the gospel must go. When this is done the church must be willing to bear the burden of their sin, nurturing them in the faith, accepting that degree of repentance which it is possible for them to achieve, looking forward to the day when through patience and love they can be free as a people from the sins of the years of their ignorance.
>
> —Doctrine and Covenants 150:10

As a result, individuals living in polygamous marriages were baptized in India, with the stipulation that no polygamous man could marry additional wives. Today, the practice is virtually unknown among the Sora church members—all because the church was willing to absorb that "stain" and bear the burden of their sin. It has been a living expression of Jesus' words: "I came not to send peace, but a sword; ... he who loseth his life for my sake will find it." Such a priority, we have learned, is a central aspect of Temple ministry.

Affirm the dignity of all people

The Turkana people of Lodwar, Kenya, have long been considered by many neighbors as worthless, hopeless drunks who spend all of their time either inebriated, brewing an illegal liquor called *changaa*, or somehow scrounging and stealing enough money to buy more grain to make more *changaa*. Their emaciated bodies, as well, were particularly susceptible to the harsh effects of *changaa* on empty bellies. That was all true, at least until Alicia Odupa and her husband Elkana, a Kenyan government official, were transferred to Lodwar.

The Odupas' lives had been changed after coming into contact with the Kenya Church about that same time. It was their testimony and effort—particularly on Alicia's part—in responding to God's Spirit in the midst of the Turkanas that a remarkable story can be told today. Alicia began to teach the women how to make baskets, and gradually they were spending less of their time with *changaa* and more in building a new life. This process has taken years and is being accomplished through much hard work, patience, and energy. It has happened because one woman dared to use her "spiritual eyes" as the first step in developing the potential of God's children who were forgotten or ignored by the rest of the world.

All are called; all are accountable

Without a doubt the opening of priesthood ordination to women has been the most divisive event for the church in recent years, perhaps even in the entire history of the Reorganization. Some of those who contended in 1984 that God *would not*, *could not* do such a thing have since left the church over this and other issues. Families, congregations, and entire jurisdictions have suffered.

Beginning at the 1984 World Conference, many on both sides appealed to the authority of scripture for precedent in deciding what the church should do. But ultimately, that has been an inadequate and inappropriate process because it ignores this basic question: Why should we do such a new thing? As Graceland professor Bob Mesle put it, in a lecture given at the Stone Church in October 1989:

> Ordaining women was a good decision. And I know that many people spent anguished hours talking, praying, and reflecting on that decision. For all of that I am grateful. But I believe we made that decision in the wrong way. We appealed to authority rather than deciding on the merits of the ideas. We relied on metaphysics rather than an examination of what would best promote the welfare of the children.
>
> —*Distinguished Author Lectures, Volume 2* (Herald House, 1990), 18

Perhaps someday Section 156 will be remembered as much or more for its emphasis on ministerial accountability than one sentence: "Therefore, do not wonder that some women of the church are being called to priesthood responsibilities." Temple ministry is both inclusive and responsible. It is open to all individuals who are willing to be accountable to God *through the church*. Such ministry cannot take place in a vacuum; it is part of the witness of this faith community. It can, as well, be likened to a journey that requires preparation and dedication.

One of the most interesting aspects of this controversy has been the gradual and growing acceptance of women's priesthood ministry throughout the church.

Repeatedly, I have heard testimonies of those who initially were completely opposed to the idea but who have since found validity in the ministry of a wife, daughter, mother, sister, aunt, grandmother, or friend. They have moved beyond seeing this in terms of a concept because the Spirit of Christ has been expressed in another's life—and they could not deny it!

Makers of peace and seekers of justice

The church's vocabulary has undergone a transformation. Where once it was rare to hear anyone speaking in the church of peace and justice, today it is almost commonplace. Two major peace workshops have been held, the first in the Kirtland Temple in 1986 and the second in the Washington, D.C., Metropole in 1989, with other such conferences now being planned in other jurisdictions.

The Kirtland Symposium tended to focus on major global issues, particularly nuclear disarmament and worldwide conflict. "Learning to Build a Peaceful World" in Washington, D.C., took a more particularized approach by dealing with peace in the context of our families, schools, churches, communities, and nation. It included recognition that the *shalom* spoken of for centuries must include living in right relationship with other people, the environment, and Divinity. This was all in keeping with the prophetic direction approved by the 1974 World Conference:

> You who are my disciples must be found continuing in the forefront of those organizations and movements which are recognizing the worth of persons and are committed to bringing the ministry of my Son to bear on their lives. Working together to this end will promote unity, resolve conflicts, relieve tensions between indi-

viduals, and heal the wounds which have been sapping the strength of the church, spiritually and materially. This you must do in the spirit of love and compassion as revealed in my Son during his journey in your midst.
—Doctrine and Covenants 151:9-10

Rely on grace

It was a memorable moment for many Saints when the flag of El Salvador was finally brought into the conference chamber at the start of the 1990 World Conference. Perhaps there is no rational explanation for the survival of the Restoration gospel in that war-torn nation. Their story has a lot to do with the dedicated efforts of Seventy Ed Guy, who many years ago left behind a more comfortable life in North America for the uncertainties of being a missionary in Central America. Often the Saints there have survived and been nurtured simply by the grace of God. It is, of course, a powerful and humbling lesson to learn how to dwell in the presence of God in the midst of human uncertainties. That has been a common thread in the church during the past three decades in particular.

This brief overview of Temple ministry development just begins to tell the story of the Saints in bringing the church to this hour. What if we could somehow go back in time thirty years to challenge the church to prepare for the Temple in this way: learn to heal the body, mind, and spirit; bear the burdens of sin; affirm the worth of all people; establish worshiping communities; call all to service and accountability; seek peace and justice; and rely on grace? Could we have borne such a cross knowingly? Or would such a challenge have been overwhelming?

The church has benefited from taking this uncertain

path. We may not know exactly where we're headed, but at least we know where we've been and what lay underneath the surface. I now like to think of the magnificent spiral-shaped structure as a 300-foot-tall "tip of the iceberg" symbolizing the intersection of divine grace and human effort.

Like the sacraments of the church, the Temple structure is becoming a visible sign of invisible grace. I eagerly join with the Saints to build this "shining symbol of God's love" and "ensign to the world of the breadth and depth of the devotion of the Saints." The Temple is so much more than any of us ever dreamed it would be.

Originally published in ***Restoration Witness*** *(Herald House, January/February 1989): 5-9.*

2
Special Place, Sacred Space

A couple of blocks from my boyhood home stood a very large, spreading tree. I don't recall what kind of tree it was—it could have been walnut, oak, or elm. We called it the "Big Tree" or, sometimes, simply "the Tree." I do remember that it represented a special place for me.

By far the biggest tree in the neighborhood, it provided a place to get away from adults and, as far as we kids in the neighborhood were concerned, a safe sanctuary. Because its limbs hung to the ground as well as stretched high into the sky, entrance to the Tree meant entering almost a different reality. Although it stood no more than a hundred yards from my home, it was in a different world. I could escape there—escape from my parents' gaze and my older brothers' interference—into an imagined existence.

Looking back now from the perspective of being a parent myself, I suspect that my mother, in particular, must have worried about me falling from the limbs of the Tree. That was not my concern when I was nine.

I have many concerns today about my own children's safety. It's not just about falling out of a tree during unsupervised play. I worry about all the dangers of urban/suburban life in the late eighties: drugs, sexual perversions, violence, pornography, alcohol abuse—things that didn't even occur to me thirty years ago.

I walked or rode my bicycle to school about a mile from home in the small town of my childhood. Although I live in the same town today, it has become a sprawling suburban area with forty times as many people. My son's elementary school is closer to home than was mine, yet my wife and I are relieved there is bus transportation now.

Understanding the Symbol

Today the Tree symbolizes for me a place of safety, a refuge, a place that encouraged my imagination and sense of adventure. Perhaps it wasn't quite as enormous as I remember it—it was uprooted to make way for a house before I left adolescence. Yet I will always remember it as the vehicle through which I could dream and dare the things which seemed unreasonable elsewhere in my neighborhood and my world.

When I was all grown up—after I had graduated from university—I still dreamed of adventure. I moved away from my hometown—more than 2,500 miles in fact—to a place that seemed even more wonderful than anything I'd dreamed about in the Tree. I discovered a new home while acting on blind faith that God's Spirit was leading me.

For six years I lived in Vancouver, British Columbia, Canada. Although it sits in one of the most spectacular places for a city anywhere in the world, bordered by water and snowcapped mountains, Vancouver's greatest beauty to me is not due to its geography. What I recall with greatest fondness are the people I met who accepted me as part of their community.

The Saints I became acquainted with in Vancouver were as different from my small-town upbringing as was the rich, cosmopolitan, ethnic mix of the city itself. Brought up in a rather traditional, highly structured church environment, I was unprepared for their openness and their risk taking, their greater emphasis on the spirit rather than the letter of most things, including the church. It was heady stuff, indeed, for a young man in his twenties finding himself and his relationship with God in a loving, caring community.

Although I've been to many other reunions, probably none will ever take the place in my memory of weeks spent with the British Columbia Saints at Samish Island on Puget Sound in Washington State. I've experienced community in many other parts of the church before and since, yet that community always will hold a special place for me. It will, in a sense, always be mine. I have friends throughout the church, but there is a difference with my friends from British Columbia. I cherish them as special sisters and brothers even though I haven't returned to Vancouver in more than eight years.

The Sacred Community

An aerial photograph of Vancouver graces one wall in my office. It is a spectacular sight: deep blue harbor, green and white mountains, sandy beaches, and the lushness of Stanley Park starkly adjacent to downtown high-rises and World's Fair pavilions. But when I look at that picture, I don't see the natural, physical beauty of the city; I see the remembered beauty of the Saints' community that I experienced. That is what makes Vancouver special for me; it is a sacred memory that helps give depth and purpose to my life.

The Temple

About a mile or so from my office at Herald House lies a large parking lot adjacent to the Auditorium. Within a few years a magnificent temple will rise on the site pointing heavenward more than 300 feet. Even now it is a special place to me. Though it does not yet exist in physical form, it exists in my mind and soul.

It is a sacred future memory just as the Big Tree and Vancouver represent sacred past memories. Already it has become an important symbol helping me understand my relationship to God and other human beings. The Temple has begun to help me visualize the living presence of Christ embodied in the Saints who will build it and use it.

When I think of the Big Tree, images of adventure, freedom, and sanctuary come to mind; Vancouver recalls some of the same things, only in much different ways. The Temple inspires me to seek spiritual adventure, freedom of my soul, and the protection and challenge of being in God's presence. It makes me wonder, it gives me hope, it challenges me to think and dream.

*Originally published in the **Saints Herald** Vol. 137, No. 4 (April 1990): 7-10.*

3

Keys of Temple Endowment

I don't go anywhere without my keys. Without them I can't unlock doors to my car, house, office, or bank safety deposit box. With them I can do all sorts of things: open many doors, go any number of places, and gain access to needed information. In that sense, keys are a wonderful metaphor for the Temple.

As a child and long before I even knew what a metaphor was, I somehow knew to connect keys with my sketchy vision of the Temple and the longed-for mystical experience of my Latter Day Saint community—the Endowment. Certainly, the many Doctrine and Covenants references to "keys of the kingdom" and "priesthood power and authority" were a part of my church vocabulary. More recently, however, I've grown uncomfortable using the devices that open locks as a primary image for the Temple and the priesthood's ministerial role.

Opening doors remains a terrific way of looking at Temple ministry. The problem comes when I realize that the keys I carry around are *mine.* Not just anybody can or should possess them. I control those keys; nobody uses them without first obtaining permission from the one who has authority over them—me (and, of course, my wife).

Keys and Control

Sociologists tell us that keys inherently involve control, authority, and power; therefore, they are typically "male" instruments. Recently, I came across a study of a modern equivalent to keys: TV and VCR remote controls.[1] Researchers state we North American men tend to take possession of remotes (interestingly, the word "control" is usually dropped) as part of our unique way of watching television. It didn't take much reading before I realized this report was not simply referring to the way *most* men and women view television; my wife and I fit the pattern.

I like to sit and watch, focusing on the task of being entertained or informed. My wife, though, usually feels the need to be doing something while sitting near a television—cross-stitching, sewing, smocking, ironing, or cutting out fabric. She frequently drops hints that I need to be doing something "useful" at such times; I usually turn a polite but deaf ear. What I sometimes find hardest to accept, like most men, is the way she breaks in on my watching with conversation.

Apparently women watch television as part of more important social acts. This, of course, clashes with us task-oriented men, whose narrow focus seeks to eliminate all distractions. Here, however, is where I part company with most men who keep their remotes handy—one for the TV and another for the VCR—so they can flick through the channels at each commercial break or whenever the mood strikes them to do so.

In a good many North American households this pattern is repeated: the husband/father controls the remote, which means he *controls* the TV and the VCR. Researchers discovered one fascinating exception: When the oldest male is unemployed and thereby replaced as the primary income provider of the household, he no longer is accorded the same measure of authority.

Lest anyone think this pattern comes solely from genes, researchers note that in many South American households, which tend to be multigenerational, the grandmother keeps the remote in her apron pocket. She is the ultimate authority who controls what is watched by everybody else.

Now, of course, watching television and using remote controls might seem to have little to do with how we will experience the Temple, and it is certainly not a direct, apt analogy in this case. However, it may help us shed new light on some important questions. For example, who has the proper authority to hold and control the "keys" of the Temple? Will the Temple experience be a narrowly focused one for individuals (after the male pattern) or more of a social situation (typically "female") requiring interaction among diverse members of a faith community? In other words, will endowment arise from *power* or *mutuality?* Will the blessings of the Temple flow *down* through a hierarchy or *out* through a faith community?

Open to All

Traditionally the church has identified priesthood as authority figures. We speak rather freely of the rights and privileges of priesthood, after all—although the responsibility and service required of these roles are increasingly acknowledged. But by identifying any one group with the power to control and exercise authority, it can become a short step to then restrict access and participation by those lacking proper credentials or worthiness. Surely the Temple should be the one place open to *all* people so they can come deliberately into the presence of Divinity.

No doubt it will take considerable effort to use the Temple in a *social* rather than a *private* way, considering how our North American culture prizes individuality—including matters of faith, experience, and relationship with God. Remember, though, that this is not supposed to be a *North American* temple.

One key to understanding the Temple in a transcultural way comes from the Apostle Paul:

> I beseech you therefore, brethren, by the mercies of God, that ye present your bodies a living sacrifice, holy, acceptable unto God, which is your reasonable service. And be not conformed to this world; but be ye transformed by the renewing of your mind, that ye may prove what that good, and acceptable, and perfect will of God is.
>
> —Romans 12:1-2

Paul goes on to speak of how, through grace, he has come to understand that individuals should not think too highly of themselves but to be "one body in Christ" whose members belong to one another. Elsewhere he writes how human beings in community can become temples, or dwelling places, for the presence of Divinity (see I Corinthians 3).

It is surprising to realize how few biblical references there are to keys. The symbolism does not appear at all in the Old Testament; in the New it refers to the ultimate power and authority delegated by God through Jesus Christ. In Matthew 16, Jesus confers keys on Peter to "bind and loose"; in Luke 11:52, the scribes are said to have failed in their role as possessors of the key of knowledge that enables humankind to enter the kingdom. The only other references come in Revelation where angels possess keys to a "bottomless pit," while

Christ alone holds the keys to the gates of heaven: "I have set before thee an open door, and no man can shut it" (Revelation 3:8). Obviously there is no need for gatekeepers. As those who stand in the stead of Christ, priesthood proclaim this open-door gospel with the power and responsibility to beckon all to come and follow Christ.

Fortunately there are many meanings for keys. Tuesday night in my family is choir night. My daughter sings with the "cherubs," my son practices with the youth choir, and my wife and I are part of the adult choir. We rehearse in different rooms at church, and the sounds from each occasionally become a distraction. This is especially true if we are singing in different keys, the basic "language" that allows male and female voices to blend in four-part harmony with instrumental accompaniment.

The key sometimes changes in the middle of an anthem, but at least we all change at the same time. If we didn't—if the tenors and sopranos sang in the key of C while the basses and altos were in E minor—the result would be a horrendous jumble of discordant sounds. Instead, the choir director leads a group that can produce unity out of diversity—harmony through the combined, unified efforts of many individuals. Sometimes the male voices get to sing the melody; occasionally we stick with the same note for measures on end. Quite often we have trouble "finding our notes" the first time we run through a song. It can take hard work to reach agreement on the right pitch, rhythm, and intonation.

Even after mastering an anthem, we still must recognize that the choir's part in a worship service is just one ingredient among many. Music can play a significant role, but it might be only a tiny part of the spiritual experience for some worshipers regardless of the time it takes up. As well, any attempt to control worshipers' responses raises the specter of manipulation and should, therefore, be avoided. There is always more than meets the eye—or ear. And *that* is a Temple "truth" with which I'm much more comfortable.

Model of Service

One of the greatest musicians of recent centuries exemplified this kind of metaphor. He is recognized as *the* most significant compiler and interpreter of Bach's organ works. In fact, some believe that many organ fugues would have been lost had it not been for this extraordinarily talented recitalist. Yet he never considered himself foremost as a musician. That was his hobby. He made his living as a philosophy professor in Europe at the turn of the twentieth century.

But something happened with the publication of his book, *The Quest for the Historical Jesus*. Others might have stumbled through a monumental faith crisis with his conclusion that the Jesus of history can *never* be known to us, forever separated by time, culture, and the filters of the early Christian communities that produced the only accounts of his life—the Gospels. Instead of losing his faith, he gave up a secure university teaching career and walked across campus to enroll in medical school along with undergraduates far younger than he. After graduating, Albert Schweitzer left Europe to open the Lambaréné Hospital in French Equatorial Africa. He continued to perform organ recitals throughout the world and write books and scholarly articles, but only to support his medical work in Africa.

His life is a model of selfless, humanitarian service, yet most people have no idea what motivated him. Biographical sketches mention his 1952 Nobel Peace Prize and briefly note his other accomplishments in philosophy, organ music, and church work. But what he did in Africa as a physician came out of the mystery of a Christ who transcends history. That encounter gave strength, purpose, and unity to everything else in Schweitzer's life. In that sense, his Christlike service was similar to the keystone in an arch. That architectural metaphor, too, is a worthy one to use in regard to the Temple.

Other Issues

After issues of control and authority, the next greatest problem with keys is that only one specific key can open a lock. Even if others *seem* to fit, they won't turn the tumblers in the necessary way. That is a desirable characteristic for a padlock; it's not so good in the Temple. It brings to mind the story of "The Magic Ring":[2]

A woman once asked her teacher, "Which is the true religion?" The teacher replied, "Once there was a special ring that everyone believed gave its bearer the gifts of grace, kindness, and generosity. When the ring's owner was on his deathbed, his three sons came separately and asked for it as an inheritance. The old man promised it to each of them. Then he instructed a skilled jeweler to make two rings identical to the original. Before the man died, he gave a ring to each son without mentioning the copies.

"Inevitably the three sons discovered the others' rings, and they appeared before the local judge to ask his help in deciding who had the true magic ring. The judge examined all three but found them to be completely alike. He then said, 'Why must anyone decide now? We shall know who has the magic ring when we observe who acts with kindness, honesty, and wisdom.'

"Now," the teacher concluded, "religions are like the three brothers in the story. The moment their members cease striving for justice, mercy, and love, we will know that their religion is not the one God gave the world."

Likewise, we will know if the Temple built in Independence is true by observing the lives of the people who use it. If they are a people who obviously have been empowered and inspired by divine grace that transforms and sends them forth as sacrificial servants—in the way of Jesus Christ—then we shall know it is God's temple. However, if those who use the Temple are concerned more with controlling the right of who goes there and the manner they experience it, then perhaps it will not, after all, be the "true" one.

The Temple, then, is not a place to exercise authority, power, and control—to proclaim, in essence, that there is only one way, *our way*, and we alone will determine exactly what happens. Nor is the Temple intended for narrowly focused, individualistic encounters with the Divine. Rather, it should be a place for communities to celebrate mutuality and bring shared needs, concerns, and hopes before God. As prophetic guidance informs us, it is to be "a place in which the essential meaning of the Restoration as healing and redeeming agent is given new life and understanding, inspired by the life and witness of the Redeemer of the world" (Doctrine and Covenants 156:5e).

Perhaps we task-oriented men who like to control situations and maintain a rigid, private focus can learn a valuable lesson from women who generally are considerably more process oriented and attuned to social matters. This could be a major gift to the church from the women's movement *if* we are willing to accept it. Is it, then, merely a coincidence that the church is called to build the Temple at the same time that the ministerial roles of priesthood have been opened to women?

We should anticipate marvelous spiritual endowment in the Temple because endowment is an experience of a prophetic *community*. The role of priesthood within that diverse, special community known as the body of Christ is probably more like choir directors than gatekeepers. The key is enablement, not control.

Endowment will occur when divine grace is matched by a humble, human desire to be like Jesus. As that process develops, the Temple experience could become the keystone of our faith community. In that day we will celebrate a new metaphor: the choirs of heaven blending their voices in harmony with diverse choirs on earth, all singing in the same key, for the glory of God and the establishment of peace on earth.

Notes

1. "Home, Home on the Remote" in Men, Myth and Media: First of a two-part series on gender and the media *Media & Values* No. 48 (Fall 1989), published by the Center for Media and Values, 1962 Shenandoah Street, Los Angeles, CA 90034.
2. "The Magic Ring," adapted from a story attributed originally to Moses Mendelsohn and retold by William R. White, *Stories for the Journey: A Sourcebook for Christian Storytellers* (Minneapolis, Minnesota: Augsburg Publishing House, 1988), 100-101.

DIALOGUE

A JOURNAL OF MORMON THOUGHT

is an independent quarterly established to express Mormon culture and to examine the relevance of religion to secular life. It is edited by Latter-day Saints who wish to bring their faith into dialogue with the larger stream of Judeo-Christian thought and with human experience as a whole and to foster artistic and scholarly achievement based on their cultural heritage. The journal encourages a variety of viewpoints; although every effort is made to ensure accurate scholarship and responsible judgment, the views expressed are those of the individual authors and are not necessarily those of The Church of Jesus Christ of Latter-day Saints or of the editors.

*Originally published in **DIALOGUE: A Journal of Mormon Thought** Vol. 24, No. 1 (Spring 1991): 87-98.*
Used with permission.

4

The Temple in Zion: A Reorganized Perspective on a Latter Day Saint Institution

Bewilderment etched the man's face. "You mean, there will be *absolutely* no rites or special ordinances *at all* in your temple. Well, then, why build it?"

Such comments may be typical of LDS responses to the RLDS Temple in Independence, Missouri—the place Joseph Smith, Jr., designated as the "Center Place of Zion." I am not surprised that Latter-day Saints have a tough time understanding what we "Reorganites" are doing with a temple. A good many RLDS—all along the spectrum from rigid traditionalists to ultra-progressives—are struggling with the idea, too. This is perhaps inevitable when divergent faith communities (both within the Reorganized Church and between RLDS and LDS) take different paths. The task of understanding each other's religion then becomes evermore difficult.

Even though we frequently share a common vocabulary, scriptures, and a mutual historical starting point, the RLDS and LDS churches now offer radically different expressions of what Joseph Smith, Jr., began more than a century and a half ago. Yet I believe both churches are *true* Latter Day Saint churches. Historically, we have equated "true" with "only," thereby failing to accept that different communities can exist in a relationship with God without forcing each to deny the validity of others. Therefore, without lapsing too deeply into a critical compare-and-contrast format (old habits are, after all, very hard to break), I will attempt the difficult task of explaining to a predominately Mormon audience why I believe we RLDS are building a temple. Of course, as a faithful member of the Reorganized Church, I cannot speak for the LDS—I can offer only what I *understand* they believe. And I can offer only *my* perspective on the Reorganized Temple, not the official perspective, belief, or doctrine of the Reorganized Church, for there are perhaps no such things. A definition of our faith can be elusive; we have no equivalent to the Articles of Faith that Mormon children learn in Primary.

It is just as difficult to pin down exactly what the temple experience will be like and how it will change the Reorganized Church and its members' spiritual life. We won't begin to know until after it is built and being used. Why, then, do we choose to build the Temple in Independence, Missouri? It is not simply because we have been commanded through divine revelation to do so. It is true that our founding prophet, Joseph Smith, Jr., first issued the call in 1833 that "an house should be built unto me [God] in the land of Zion" (RLDS Doctrine and Covenants 94:3a; LDS Doctrine and Covenants 97:7)[1] and the prophetic vision was updated in more recent years by two of his prophetic successors in the Reorganized Church. W. Wallace Smith recorded this revelation in April 1968:

> The time has come for a start to be made toward building my temple in the Center Place. It shall stand on a portion of the plot of ground set apart for this purpose many years ago by my servant Joseph Smith, Jr. The shape and character of the building is to conform to ministries which will be carried out within its walls. ... It is also to be noted that the full and complete use of the temple is yet to be revealed but that there is no provision for secret ordinances now or ever. ...
>
> —RLDS Doctrine and Covenants 149:6a; 149A:6[2]

Sixteen years later, in April 1984, Wallace B. Smith received revelation that further clarified the purpose of an RLDS temple:

> The temple shall be dedicated to the pursuit of peace. It shall be for reconciliation and for healing of the spirit. It shall also be for a strengthening of faith and preparation for witness. By its ministries an attitude of wholeness of body, mind, and spirit as a desirable end toward which to strive will be fostered. It shall be the means for providing leadership education for priesthood and member. And it shall be a place in which the essential meaning of the Restoration as healing and redeeming agent is given new life and understanding, inspired by the life and witness of the Redeemer of the world. Therefore, let the work of planning go forward, and let the resources be gathered in, that the building of my temple may be an ensign to the world of the breadth and depth of the devotion of the Saints.
>
> —RLDS Doctrine and Covenants 156:5-6[3]

Obviously building a temple at the literal and figurative center of our faith community requires more than simply "doing what we're told," even if the source of our instructions is Divinity. After all, we are not automatons marching in lockstep to an intelligence separate from our own. God in Christ is "in us" as we become co-creators and fellow sojourners in the redemptive plan of the world's salvation. The eternal purpose in RLDS temple building is related not to an other-worldly realm but to the redemptive, healing, peacemaking, reconciling ministry of Christ in *this* world. We hope to glorify the one God of the universe through participation in the divine plan of the cause of Zion.

Let me explore some reasons why we are building this Temple.

Encounter Christ

When I was a boy, I learned about the Second Coming of Jesus Christ through the perspective of my grandmother and my traditional Reorganized Church congregation in eastern Jackson County, Missouri. My understanding was completely literal: The resurrected Jesus would come floating down out of the clouds and land at the front door of the Temple on the temple lot—a small acreage separating the RLDS Auditorium (a structure similar to the Salt Lake Tabernacle) from the Reorganized Church's largest congregation, the Stone Church. (For those unfamiliar with the area, the Mormon Visitors' Center is directly to the southeast; the RLDS Temple is being built directly north of the visitors' center.)

I envisioned this millennial Independence Temple as a near clone of the Kirtland Temple with, of course, its main entrance facing east. After entering through that east door, the resurrected Jesus would take up physical residence for a thousand years while the world beat a path to his door. The heathen nations would recognize, finally, that the RLDS should rightfully be put in charge of everything because we possessed the one true and now restored faith with the priesthood power and authority lacking in all other churches. I can clearly remember my grandmother gently persuading me to reconsider my dream of becoming a doctor—you see, there would be no need for medical practitioners during those thousand years, and there was no question that the Temple would be built in my lifetime.

She was at least right about the latter, but my late-1950s world view has undergone some changes. I no longer look for the Second Coming in such a narrow, literal way. My beliefs changed, partly because I have since rejected that apocalyptic and millennialist panorama. It conflicts with too many basic scientific realities. As well, firsthand experience with religious pluralism has tempered my belief in the One True Church. I have developed a respect for the beliefs and "temples" of others, and in doing so have reexamined the meaning of a temple for me and for my faith community. But if I no longer expect a resurrected, returned Jesus to walk into the Independence Temple, how then do I connect that holy place with the idea of a Second Coming?

The Temple is becoming a symbol for the Reorganized Church of its relationship with the Creator and creation. But that relationship, that connection with our roots, is not based primarily on our past—or humankind's past. (This may be an essential difference between the temple experience for our two churches. I am told that some LDS members faithfully attend their temple for that sense of connectedness, even though they may have set aside the more official theological meanings of the vicarious ordinances.) I am beginning to sense that the Temple for us RLDS will be a touchstone of the way we understand our *being*; in other words, it will be the central symbol of the cosmic Christ incarnating or coming in us. That's the sort of thing that is tough to channel into ritual, and I hope we never try. But it is appropriate to have a place of special renewal and empowerment where our lives can change direction and begin to more fully reflect the ministry of Jesus, who provides us a pattern. Therefore, I cannot see the "millennial ministry of Jesus Christ" as coming from one individual in the Temple. Rather, "one body in Christ" will honor the temple as its soul.

Also, I no longer expect Christ to "come again" to the Temple because I realize that in one sense, the Second Coming has already happened: I have encountered Christ in many different people—Anglicans, Catholics, Presbyterians, Mormons, Jews, Canadians, Americans, Africans, women, children, men, and (dare I say it) a secular humanist or two. Why limit the Spirit of Christ to a single body, human or divine? As a Reorganized Christian, I reject the notion that Divinity has a body just like mine, along with the idea that Christ has a specific gender, race, or nationality.

Jesus of Nazareth was a Jew who lived in ancient Palestine. But I do not believe Jesus of Nazareth is the fullness of Christ. Neither is the resurrected Jesus encountered by Saul on his way to Damascus. And of course, the central theological message of the Book of Mormon narrative is that Christ cannot be limited by time or space but can find expression outside the culture of ancient Palestine. God wears many faces. It is something like actors in a Greek drama who use different masks to change quickly from one persona or character to the next, yet the being behind the mask is the same, even though the audience perceives a separateness and uniqueness. This same idea was the original intention of early Christian theologians who spoke of the three "personas" of the Godhead. Over the centuries, the word "persons" was substituted, and that means quite a different thing. Perhaps the most important element here is the human perception involved rather than the essence of the being behind the mask.

At the Edge of Our Frontier

The frontiers of the 1990s and beyond are far different from those of the early to mid-1800s. A century and a half ago, the frontier meant the edge of unexplored or unsettled land masses, the end of civilization and the beginning of wilderness. Our frontiers today, however, are not so much matters of space and time as of being, of discovering the unknown within us, both as individuals and communities.

Joseph Smith, Jr., challenged the Saints to begin building the kingdom of God on earth by building a New Jerusalem first in Kirtland, Ohio, then in both Independence and Far West, Missouri, before the Saints finally settled along the Illinois banks of the Mississippi River in Nauvoo. Unquestionably the rough yet bustling trading town of Independence represented the American frontier in 1831 when Joseph first visited it. But like Kirtland, that latter-day New Jerusalem was set amid gentile neighbors. Joseph dreamed of a new order, yet the vision paid scant attention to gentile wishes and realities. The Saints eventually left both Kirtland and Independence after more than a little prodding by neighbors. Caldwell and Daviess counties in northern Missouri allowed a little more isolation. However, "gentiles" were there, too, and strife was not long in coming.

But the more isolated Nauvoo setting was different, coming as it did after years of persecution and religious experimentation. It provided an opportunity for further evolution of church practices and kingdom building. The Kirtland Temple had been primarily a place of public worship, a school for priesthood and members, and the headquarters for church administration. Joseph's plans for the Independence Temple were similar, but they expanded the single, Kirtland-like structure to twenty-four buildings that included space for the First Presidency and other leading quorums, for what was to become the Relief Society, and for a storehouse. Of course, those buildings were never built, even though the Saints purchased and dedicated about sixty-three acres of land before they were driven out of the county in late 1833. Even though Joseph's vision of a frontier Zion—the New Jerusalem—changed, a temple always remained central in his plans.

The variety of historical models for the Temple may lead us to wonder which will be the "right kind" of temple for the Reorganization in the 1990s. Should we copy the pattern for Kirtland, Independence, Far West, or Nauvoo? But the question is fundamentally wrong; all were right for their time and place. Therefore, the Independence Temple built by the Reorganized Church in the 1990s should not seek historical precedent, even though it will incorporate historical elements. Above all, it must be a temple for its time and place and institution—to actualize the dreams of the Saints. As a sacred space where all cultures can be at home, the Temple must be at the figurative center of its faith community and must offer a vision of the cause of Zion appropriate for its day.

A New Jerusalem today must take into account more than a single city. It certainly cannot be limited to just one religious group, nor can it attempt the kind of economic, political, social, and theological separateness of Nauvoo, Joseph's "City Beautiful," which served as the forerunner for the nation/state of Deseret. Even the LDS church was forced, eventually, to scale back the political scope of what was left of Deseret by accepting the 1890 Manifesto.

Our perspective today is much like that of the astronauts who first walked on the moon more than twenty years ago. Until that time, our horizons had been limited by how far up the side of the mountain we climbed or how far into the atmosphere our planes soared. But when we stood on the moon with those astronauts and looked out on a new horizon, we saw for the first time our beautiful blue-and-white planet hanging in the darkness of space. In a spiritual sense we saw Zion for the first time, too, encompassing the entire globe. And we finally realized (notwithstanding the work of scientific pioneers like Galileo, Copernicus, and Newton) that it is the Creator and not creation that provides the axis of the universe. This expanded and glorious vision of Zion will have a temple at its center, serving as the crossroads of divine grace and human experience.

Empowered for Service

Old Testament imagery of the Israelites' wilderness tabernacle and the New Testament concept of human communities as temples of the Holy Spirit are equally important in the RLDS Temple. In Moses' time, the Hebrew tribes reserved a special place, the Tabernacle or Tent of Meeting, for their prophet's deliberate encounters with Yahweh, the God of their forebears. When Moses entered the tent, the pillar of smoke and fire, which hovered over the Israelite encampment day and night as a symbol of divine presence, descended. Hidden within the smoke, Yahweh spoke to Moses, then ascended into the heavens. With his face covered to protect his people from its brightness, Moses left the tent to let the Israelites know just what Yahweh wanted them to do. His experience with Yahweh was not so much a weighing in the balance of the good and evil deeds of his people but rather a realization that through all the Israelites' experiences, they were still God's chosen ones with a particular mission.

God is no longer hidden within smoke and fire as in Old Testament times but is revealed in the light of a new day—in the persona of Jesus Christ—without the need for a structure in which God could temporarily "tabernacle." As the writer of John's Gospel wrote (drawing on the same Greek words used in the Septuagint version of the Exodus story), "The Word was made flesh [and] *lived among us*" (literally, "pitched his tent among us") (John 1:14).[4] The New Testament writers extended the idea that the presence of God in Christ would "encamp" *within* believers as their communities assumed the function of temples. Most orthodox Christians therefore no longer see a need for any kind of structural temple.

Yet perhaps because we Latter Day Saints have always drawn on Old Testament symbols, we have been temple builders. Like Moses, we sense the need to approach Divinity to discern what we are to do. But we in the Reorganized Church should not depend on our prophet to represent us for those deliberate encounters, although in some cases that may happen. As a prophetic community we must go to the Temple in unity for insight and empowerment. Perhaps our Temple experience will challenge us to grow beyond our reliance on the prophet. This new perspective can offer expanded spiritual horizons, stretching us to see the world's need for God's community, which offers compassionate, humble service in the name of Jesus Christ.

I don't expect to "see Jesus" in the literal sense in the Temple. However, I am confident that we will "experience Christ" in ways and forms heretofore unimaginable. That experience cannot come through mere ritual or reenactment of someone else's story, nor can it originate in our own efforts. It must come through grace as God's involvement in the world is met by our selfless service to other human beings and to all of creation. We can "feel good" (awed, inspired, thrilled, challenged, humbled, lifted up) in the holy setting of the Temple, but unless we return to our homes empowered with an expanded testimony of God's love and purpose for creation, the experience serves no lasting purpose. We are like Apostle Paul's Corinthian cymbals and gongs.

Keys of the Kingdom

The term "keys of the kingdom" is used frequently in our movement, often in regard to priesthood ministry and responsibility. The Kirtland Saints were the first to think of their "House of the Lord" as the place of endowment of such keys. The Nauvoo Saints also used similar terminology about their temple, although the theological underpinning had evolved dramatically by that time to become the ritual observances virtually guaranteeing celestial glory through a step-by-step process, perhaps borrowed in some way from Masonic rites. Perhaps we in the Restoration movement have been impoverished, though, by thinking of these "keys of the kingdom" almost solely as mechanical devices used to open doors. While the symbolism is appropriate, it has limitations. Used *only* in this way, they lose their metaphorical power, becoming things to acquire by doing all the right acts in front of the proper authorities.

Several other metaphors can inform RLDS Temple practice in a much broader sense. The keystone of an arch is the one stone that not only completes the arch's shape but gives strength to the entire structure. Seen in this way, the Temple in Zion is what has been missing in the Reorganized Church; it will give shape, character, and strength to everything we do in proclaiming the gospel of Christ to a world that groans for redemption. To extend the metaphor, the key in a musical score is vital to keep all the various instruments and voices in harmony. The church is neither a choir singing in unison nor a jumble of miscellaneous noises, each straining to be heard above the din. Members of the body of Christ do not all do the same things or make the same sounds, yet the mysterious blend of our combined efforts achieves the desired end. The Temple could provide the key to unify the church the same way that music written in the same key for different instruments can transform mere sound into Beethoven's Fifth Symphony. Scientists refer to this as synergism; I call it Temple ministry.

One obvious characteristic of ministry in the early decades of the Restoration movement—in general and specifically related to temples—was male dominance. The authority, power, and control of an all-male priesthood played a major role in theology and church administration. Perhaps we should accept that dominance merely as part of nineteenth-century American culture. But it is not at all appropriate at the dawn of the twenty-first century. Therefore, the Reorganized Church's Temple ministry, I contend, must not be based on such blatantly male images but should reflect the empowerment that flows from mutuality and equality. The church needs to follow the inspired counsel of a prophetic community more than the accepted authority and control of a male-dominated hierarchical structure which, in turn, supports its leading role with scripture that arises from an even more patriarchal era.

In 1984 our RLDS prophet Wallace B. Smith made a crucial step to bring the will of God to the Reorganized Church by extending the call of priesthood ministry: "I say to you now, as I have said in the past, that all are called according to the gifts which have been given them. This applies to priesthood as well as to any other aspects of the work. Therefore, do not wonder that some women of the church are being called to priesthood responsibilities. This is in harmony with my will" (RLDS Doctrine and Covenants 156:9b-c).

Some RLDS members contend that God would not or could not do such a "new thing" and have separated themselves from the main body of the Reorganized Church. At the same time, the more than 3,000 women who have been ordained have added a new and vital aspect to the church's ministry as Christ's servants and burden bearers. For those who "have eyes to see," that should be ample evidence that God *does* do new things. Sadly, some choose not to see; and there is division, brokenness, and enmity in our midst.

Center of Healing and Reconciliation

When you are sick, you go to a doctor, who prescribes treatment (medicine, bed rest, exercise, change of habits), and you are "cured." Remember, though, that Jesus didn't cure everybody who came to him. He frequently told even those he did heal not to tell anybody else. They rarely obeyed, however, and so he often was inundated with curiosity seekers who hampered his other ministry.

If the Temple became a "healing shrine," there is a risk that hordes of the curious, as well as the sick, might prevent it from offering other kinds of vitally important service. Perhaps those with chronic, rather than acute, illnesses might be served better in the Temple. But should they expect to be "cured" according to the acute-disease model, especially considering that the nature of their illnesses is completely different?

I have a friend who has multiple sclerosis. He is in his thirties, faced with a chronic condition that is also progressive. We don't get to see one another much because we now live more than 2,000 miles apart. Some time ago I visited his home for the first time in nine years. Although I could stay only one night, he gently reminded me after greeting me warmly that it was time for his afternoon rest. If he did not lie down for about forty-five minutes, our planned evening get-together at a mutual friend's home would undoubtedly place a strain on his health and well-being. In short, his MS might flare up if he did not take the time to recharge his energy.

I marveled at his self-discipline. It was a poignant reminder of the different meaning health and wholeness has for him. I wish I had the same level of self-discipline in dealing with my own chronic medical condition. In the twenty years I have lived with Crohn's disease, an inflammatory bowel disease, I have experienced numerous valleys and peaks. Slowly I have come to realize the relativity of healing and wholeness. I don't expect to walk into the Temple in Zion someday to have my Crohn's disease healed any more than I'd expect to have the lengthy, surgically removed portions of my small intestine suddenly grow back. Yet the discipline of the Temple may open new vistas of the meaning of healing and reconciliation as inner qualities and outward activities.

One aspect of reconciliation is peace. The RLDS Temple is dedicated to the pursuit of peace. This neither supplants the gospel of Jesus Christ, nor is it an end result. A pursuit implies an ongoing process. My grandmother was not alone in believing the peaceable era envisioned by Isaiah and others as an absence of sickness and discord. But Christ's kingdom on earth will have continual need of healers, reconcilers, and advocates. Can we not see that kingdom as an "end" without placing everything on a timeline? The Temple could transcend such time/space limitations. Peace, in Christ's kingdom, will become more akin to the Hebrew *shalom* and less an existence to look forward to in "the sweet by and by."

Inclusive Ministry

Certainly we RLDS may be tempted to take pride in our efforts, especially once the magnificent spiral-shaped sanctuary begins to rise three times the height of the Auditorium across the street. RLDS members and friends of the church will come to Independence by the thousands to view this unique structure, built by a relatively small group that frequently is racked by internal dissention and disagreement. The Temple is sure to become many things to many people. We have just begun to explore its role as a planetary symbol, facilitator, sacred space, and advocate for peace in the twenty-first-century church and world. We have a long way to go before all of God's children will feel welcome in the Temple.

The Temple may encourage many to respond to the call to follow Christ. After all, this Temple belongs to Christ and will stand as a beacon of Christ's way, which, as scripture tells us, is the way to know God. But it is not a road map owned exclusively by Latter Day Saints. It is not marked by specific rituals guaranteeing celestial glory. Jesus, always open to divine grace as healer, reconciler, peacemaker, witness, and humble servant, offers us a glimpse of God's way. He shows us that God is willing to lift us from our human brokenness because of the unmeasurable mystery of divine love. And we are to be like Jesus. At the Temple, we will learn to do that.

Focal Point for Our Future

More than 150 years ago, Joseph Smith prophetically called his people to build the Temple in Zion. We have begun the task of raising the Temple as an "ensign of peace" near the very spot from which he spoke. Is it mere coincidence that this place now also represents something quite the opposite from what he envisioned? A few miles from Jackson County, Missouri, some 150 underground missile silos sit amid the fertile farmland of western Missouri. At ground level they appear to be nothing more than fenced enclosures about 150 feet square, containing a large concrete slab and a protruding doorway. Beneath each enclosure, however, sits a gigantic intercontinental missile armed with multiple nuclear warheads, each many times more potent than those dropped on Japan in 1945.

The missiles are aimed at targets in the Soviet Union, ready to be fired, our political and military leaders tell us, in response to nuclear attack. The command center for these missile silos is at Whiteman Air Force Base about fifty miles southeast of Independence. Additional preparations are underway these days to house the newest, most controversial, and most expensive ($525 million apiece) weapon in U.S. military history: the B-2 (Stealth) Bomber. Unfortunately the Persian Gulf crisis may keep the B-2 from being cancelled or cut back.

What this all means is that Jackson County, Missouri, sits essentially at "ground zero" for the start of World War III and the possible end of humankind as we know it. But the site for the Temple also can become the starting point for Christ's kingdom and the peaceable era that prophets have envisioned for centuries. By building the Temple, we can respond positively to the choice offered first to Joshua: "I have set before you life and death, blessing and cursing; therefore choose life, that both thou and thy seed may live" (Deuteronomy 30:19).

At the Crossroads

Israel, the Promised Land for Yahweh's chosen people, was at the center of several ancient trading routes. A cosmopolitan mix of merchants and warriors interacted with a people that otherwise may have remained a tiny and obscure footnote to history. But instead Israel has profoundly influenced at least the Western world's religious, moral, ethical, and philosophical thought. It rose to its greatest political and economic glory during a brief interval between the dominant eras of ancient superpowers. Who would have thought that a quarrelsome band of ex-slaves who took forty years to complete a three-week trek from Egypt to Canaan would end up influencing the world as it did? But, of course, their world position came not from business or political acumen but because they remained, by and large, faithful to their divinely appointed task.

Our calling today is not to be an updated version of ancient Israel. There is no need for such an elitist notion of divine chosenness. As well, there is no need to turn the world's peoples into clones of rich, success-oriented Westerners. The easy answers and rituals that can turn attention away from human need and misery provide the wrong path. And, of course, it is time to abolish subservient roles for women along with the autocratic hierarchies (usually patriarchal) which spawn oppression.

The world today does need Christ. And that, in brief, is why I believe God has challenged us to do a new thing by building this temple. It is the response of the Reorganized Church to God's grace, as well as a symbol of God's divine love. It is a way to connect the peoples of the Third World with those of the First and Second without oppressing or corrupting anyone. It is a place to encounter God in Christ and then to go forth to build and transform communities which express that incarnation. It is a place to carry our past with us as we look to the future. It is God's sacred place and our sacred place and, most important of all, the world's sacred place. Joseph Smith, Jr., first issued the call to build the Temple. But we can transcend his vision as we are touched by Divinity and challenged by our world's needs. Our task will be to do what Apostle Paul counseled long ago: "By the mercies of God, ... present your bodies a living sacrifice, holy, acceptable unto God, which is your reasonable service. And be not conformed to this world; but be ye transformed by the renewing of your mind, that ye may prove what that good, and acceptable, and perfect will of God is" (Romans 12:1-2).

And so, I look forward to the day that is coming soon when I can stand in the Temple with my sisters and brothers to encounter Christ who will then send us away a changed people. We then shall be, finally, a Temple people—the people of God.

Notes

1. This revelation was given through Joseph Smith, Jr., on 2 August 1833, in Kirtland; word had not yet reached Ohio of the 23 July agreement forced on the Saints in Independence to leave Jackson County.
2. This was the first direction in recent times to the Reorganized Church to build a temple in Independence. It caught a good many church members by surprise, because the Conference that year had been embroiled in a controversy over the role of the bishopric, a debate that greatly overshadowed any thought of building a temple.
3. This revelation is best remembered for opening priesthood roles to women.
4. See especially the Jerusalem Bible.

*Originally published in **Restoration Studies IV,** edited by Marjorie Troeh (Independence, Missouri: Herald Publishing House, 1988): 13-20.*

5

Temple Ministries within the RLDS Covenant Community

The concept of covenant community in the RLDS Church of today has its roots interwoven in the Latter Day Saint movement, the New Testament church, and ancient Israel. The Temple is at its center, both literally and symbolically.

In ancient Israel the holy of holies was the innermost room of the Jerusalem Temple. To non-Israelites the room was barren and empty (except in its earliest days when it housed the Ark of the Covenant, which held the tablets of the Law of Moses). But to Israel the room signified the residence of Almighty God on earth. Although the divine presence could be felt anywhere at anytime, God could be counted on to be there in the Temple always. Such a belief was both a comfort to the Israelites and a symbol of their calling as God's chosen ones. It reminded them of their desert experience when God, manifested as a cloud of smoke and a pillar of fire, led them onward. Their prophet, Moses, and their high priest, Aaron, guided them on their journey toward the Promised Land. While it might take quite awhile to get there, they knew they would reach it, because God was faithful.

Theological Symbol

It is recorded in the Gospel accounts[1] that the Temple veil separating the holy of holies from the outer courts was torn apart at the time of Jesus' crucifixion. As an expression of belief by the early Christian Church, this was more of a theological account than a literal one. But it signified, among other things, that the presence of God could not be confined to a particular place. Those early believers understood that the holy of holies—the divine presence—was embodied first in Christ Jesus and then in the body of Christ (Paul's term for the church community) so the reality of God's love might be expressed fully throughout the world.

A latter-day holy of holies should also signify the presence of Almighty God on earth; it too is more than just a room in a specific building. It is evidenced by the *cause of Zion* as expressed in Temple ministries dedicated to peace. To some "outsiders" that cause may seem as incomprehensible as ancient Israel's holy of holies did to the conquering Babylonians. To RLDS members Temple ministries that bring the reconciling, restoring Spirit of God are very real and symbolize that although God can be anywhere at anytime—and involved in diverse ways with a great many different people—the divine presence is in this work in a unique way.

This kind of ministry is directed to the living, not the dead; the focus is on feeding the hungry, clothing the naked, housing the homeless, reconciling the separated, and mediating in the midst of enmity. For that is the kind of real world in which our Savior has called us to bear the burdens of sins and to provide an affirmative witness of God's love for all creation. It is in Temple ministries that we experience the awesome presence of God, continually leading us through the "wilderness of sin" by the promise of eternal salvation. We will not come to the Temple merely to *hear* God's word or to *feel* the divine presence, although we will undoubtedly do both. We will come to the Temple to learn to *do* God's will and *become* the living, human expression of the Word, as Jesus of Nazareth was the "Word made flesh."

Sacrificial Ministry

Such Temple ministry is appropriately sacrificial in nature. An understanding of it is grounded in both the example of the ancient Jerusalem Temple and the Atonement of Jesus Christ.

Ancient Israel's sacrifices were different from those of neighboring nature and fertility religions, which based their sacrifices on the cycles of nature so the seasons would change, crops would grow, women would be fertile, the rains would fall, or the floodwaters would dry up. The sacrifices offered by the priests in the Jerusalem Temple, however, were based on a historical covenant relationship between the One God of all creation and a chosen people—Israel.

After slitting the throat of the sacrificial animal, the Israelite priest drained its blood into large bowls to sprinkle it on the inner-court altar, on the veil in front of the holy of holies, and then on the four corners of the large altar in front of the Temple, while the animal's carcass was consumed totally by fire. Such an extensive use of blood in sacrificial offerings was unique to the Israelites, who considered it to represent God's gift of life. They believed blood sacrifice atoned for the sins of the one making the sacrifice (or the entire nation of Israel on the annual Day of Atonement). If God accepted the sacrifice, the Israelites believed their sins would be ritualistically covered by the blood, leaving only their faithful obedience to the Law (Torah) as a basis for divine judgment. The offering of sin sacrifice was evidence of Israel's faithfulness; God's faithfulness to the promise and covenant was shown in scripture by a long series of saving acts. Israel, then, could be considered righteous (or justified) because of the faithfulness of both God *and* the chosen people.

The Apostle Paul used remarkably similar imagery in describing the sacrifice (Atonement) of Jesus Christ. Temple sacrifice, as known and practiced by the Israelites for centuries, became irrelevant to the salvation process. With the blood of Jesus Christ "covering" the sins of the entire world, all of humanity would be offered the possibility of being considered righteous (or justified), this time because of God's faithfulness in sending the Only Begotten *and* the response of believing obedience by all people. Such believers are referred to in several of Paul's letters as the body of Christ because through their baptism and celebration of the Lord's Supper (so they might *remember* the spilling of the Lord's blood and the breaking of his body), they participate and share ritually in this act as a living sacrifice.

> Now ye are the body of Christ, and members in particular. —I Corinthians 12:27

> I beseech you therefore, brethren, by the mercies of God, that ye present your bodies a living sacrifice, holy, acceptable unto God, which is your reasonable service. And be not conformed to this world; but be ye transformed by the renewing of your mind, that ye may prove

what that good, and acceptable, and perfect will of God is.
—Romans 12:1-2

The early Christians understood that the blood of Jesus Christ was "too heavy" for the Temple veil, covered as it was by the blood of centuries of sacrificial animals. For Christians, the Temple was no longer a place of true sacrifice (or, as previously noted, a place able to contain the divine presence). Acceptable sacrifice could occur only in the lives of believers who consider their bodies as temples.

For ye are the temple of the living God; as God hath said, I will dwell in them, and walk in them; and I will be their God, and they shall be my people.
—II Corinthians 6:16

Latter-day Temple Builders

Yet early in the development of the Latter Day Saint religion came the call to build a temple or "House of the Lord." Mainstream Christians have sometimes used this as so-called proof of Christian heresy among Latter Day Saints. Such a criticism shows a basic misunderstanding of the theological basis for this new covenant community, which has its roots in both Old and New Testaments, but which has evolved in a new way.

As Jan Shipps has pointed out in her landmark book, *Mormonism: The Story of a New Religious Tradition*, the Latter Day Saint movement is indeed a new religion—not simply a fascinating subculture within orthodox Christianity—that combines the concepts of "new Israel" and "Church of Christ" in a unique blend.[2] This covenant community, therefore, is *more than* Israel and *not just* the body of Christ. As such there is an essential, central role to be played by Temple ministries. Unlike ancient Israel, the focus is not on a building but on a growing, endowing ministry that eventually requires organization and facilities for its complete development. Unlike the New Testament church, this temple is more than an inward, symbolic concept and involves concrete involvement in the actual structures of society.

Obviously Temple ministries are not something brand new. In many cases they will appear to be what we have been doing in ministry for a long time. The unique difference will come with the sharpened focus offered by Temple facilities and the understanding that what we do sacrificially in and for the world *is* the divine presence at work.

Such an understanding of Temple ministry is in line with the admonition expressed by Joseph Smith, Jr., in December 1832 in regard to the "House of the Lord" that was to be built in Kirtland, Ohio, with corresponding implications for Independence, Missouri. The Saints were to

> prepare every needful thing, and establish a house, even a house of prayer, a house of fasting, a house of faith, a house of learning, a house of glory, a house of order, a house of God. —Doctrine and Covenants 85:36b

Preliminary plans and sketches were prepared at that time for some twenty-four structures that would provide Temple functions on the sixty-three-acre site known as the "temple lot" in Independence. They were never constructed because of mob violence and the forced eviction of Saints from Jackson County in 1833.

Evolutionary Practice

The conceptual role of temples within the Latter Day Saint movement changed significantly after this time period and reflected much of the changing theological speculations of Joseph Smith, Jr., and other church leaders. A great many of those speculations have been rejected over the years by the RLDS Church as inconsistent with what it holds as the true intent of the Restoration movement. There need be no compulsion to include them within plans for temple building today. Likewise, it would be as inappropriate and fruitless to define RLDS Temple ministry by comparison to the esoteric rites of Mormon temples as it is to define the RLDS Church itself as "not Mormon."

It is significant that the original name for the Kirtland structure was the "House of the Lord," for this temple had a far different function than its predecessor in Jerusalem. This should not be surprising considering that the Saints of the early 1830s understood themselves more in New Testament terms than in Old Testament ones. But this began to change by mid-decade, so that by Nauvoo their theocratic covenant community was less and less a "democratic body of Christ" and more and more an "authoritarian new Israel."

The theological underpinnings were changing as well. The Kirtland Temple represented some overt Old Testament understandings of divine presence and sacrifice. They were present, most importantly, in the experiences of the Saints in Kirtland. For example, their sacrificial activity in building the structure led to an outpouring of spiritual manifestations—or divine presence—at the dedication services. The Old Testament meanings found in the building at Kirtland were more subtle than in Nauvoo, although the Kirtland interior is dominated by Aaronic and Melchisedec priesthood pulpits. The washings and anointings introduced by Joseph Smith, as well, presaged Nauvoo and were reminders of ancient Israelitish practice.

The Nauvoo Temple, situated in the center—physically and symbolically—of a different kind of community, represented a notable theological development. This temple became the site of elaborate endowment rituals (oaths, sealing ceremonies, dramas) and symbolic sacrifice (most notably baptizing proxies for the dead, who, it was believed, depended on this vicarious reenactment of Christ's death and resurrection to make them clean and worthy enough to obtain celestial glory).

As well, the Nauvoo Saints believed that when they were within the temple's walls, they were, in a peculiar sense, as close to heaven on earth as possible. Such basic understandings continue to undergird temple concepts in the Utah church. The Reorganization, however, came into being in reaction to this and other elements.

Community Orientation

It is important, also, to look at the relationship of Latter Day Saint *community* to the larger society in which it has existed throughout church history. The earliest Latter Day Saints were mostly New Englanders predisposed to communitarian ideas. Their heritage of town meetings and group-oriented society dates to the earliest years of North American colonization. The Saints combined this with strong religious overtones, not the least of which was an Old Testament-type prophet who literally could speak the word of God and expect nearly unanimous support. Is it any wonder, then, that the Saints ran into trouble in Ohio and Missouri, where the "gentiles" (a divisive term in itself) represented the epitome of frontier democracy and the rugged individualism that continues to exemplify much of American society even today?

The Saints were spectacularly unsuccessful in co-existing with the southern society of Jackson County in the 1830s, and they repeated the process in northern Missouri and Nauvoo. Their concept of a separate, covenant community in the first half of the nineteenth century simply could not be tolerated in American society, much less influence it for the better. But that community of Saints as it ultimately developed in Nauvoo left the United States for the West and carved out an unusual and fascinating history. Both strains of Latter Day Saints still look to Nauvoo for meaning. One remembers Nauvoo as the pattern for a developing kingdom, the other as a debacle precipitating church reorganization.

By and large it was the more democratically oriented individuals in the church who gathered within the Reorganization. They rejected the Nauvoo concept of community (and eventually much of its theological base as well, although this took a long time and, for some RLDS, may not be complete yet). Their religion, however, was still not as individualistic as the larger Christian community. It was certainly less "chosen people" than *koinonia* (within a Latter Day Saint context) yet quite different from Christian orthodoxy.

The Reorganization

There was no temple in the Reorganization of the late-nineteenth and early-twentieth centuries (the Kirtland structure functioned more or less as a meeting hall). The RLDS Church was too busy being "not Mormon" to spend much time, effort, or money on such a dream. Instead, the church has had to deal with many crucial questions: democracy and autocracy within a theocratic order; the role of presidency; the functioning of priesthood, especially the role of bishops and now female priesthood members; and the relationship of the church as a special, covenant community within a pluralistic Christian community and the world at large. Through it all, amazingly, has survived a dream of Zion and the Temple.

Now, at the end of the twentieth century, the church is beginning to embark on building the Temple—a concept that remains at the center of this faith community. Before 1960 the RLDS Church gave only scant consideration to a temple—there was insufficient money for such a project, anyway. More importantly, there was an inadequate theological basis for it in such an inward-oriented organization.

It has been almost three decades since the beginning of the watershed decade of the 1960s when the church began seriously to look beyond itself. Not coincidentally, this is when the RLDS Church began to enter non-English-speaking cultures in a major way. The church has made significant strides in breaking away from its predominate remnant theology of earlier years (the One True Church being its catch phrase) with a strong apocalyptic emphasis (a literal Second Coming of Jesus to Independence, Missouri, ushering in the end of the world). Slowly shedding a historical rationale for its existence, the RLDS Church has begun to grapple with an incarnational approach that places it uniquely within the pluralism of Christianity and the entire world. In other words, we RLDS are beginning to see our purpose and calling less in terms of our history (as fascinating and intriguing as it is) and our set of doctrines and beliefs as in how God, in Jesus Christ, is *in* us. The emphasis is on divine calling rather than authority, leaven rather than light, process rather than end result. The theological understandings of Temple ministries at the heart of this community must reflect this.

Contrast in the Church

There are at least two contrasting views of the Temple in the RLDS Church today. Many Saints long for a temple because it represents a secure place in a Zion that is a holy city of refuge for God's chosen—and perfect—Saints. Others see absolutely no need for a temple when the millions of dollars that will be required to build such an edifice could be better spent elsewhere, especially in social ministries. There is a pressing need to reconcile these viewpoints.

Of course, the importance of the Temple lies not in a building in Jackson County, Missouri—or perhaps more properly, in buildings located throughout the world in which Temple ministries are facilitated. Rather, the importance is in the endowing ministries that shall come through this community for the benefit of the world and *from* the world to enrich the church. Out of the Temple will come a community that embodies the divine presence in spiritual and physical ways to sacrificially bear the burden of the sins of the world. Thus, divine sovereignty can be restored within the persons and other elements of society. Temple structures (both physical and organizational) will facilitate this as Saints—and others—come to the House of the Lord to be trained, empowered, uplifted, and ennobled, all of which can lead to an ever-increasing endowment of Christlike ministry. True, the church has already attempted to minister in this way. But it has consistently fallen short, perhaps because there has been no symbolic or physical temple at the center of its community.

The institution of the church is in a curious position. It is a community-oriented organization that exists, predominately, in the individualistic society of North America. Although the interaction between this faith community and society-at-large need not repeat the example of Jackson County, Far West, and Nauvoo in the 1830s and 1840s, there may well be limits to the possible numerical expansion of the church in North America. Church and culture operate differently; the church offers a message in a community context to a society that still worships the individual. In other cultures, however, such is not the case. In those societies with a strong community orientation, such as Haiti and parts of Africa and India, the RLDS Church has already begun to flourish. We RLDS usually point with pride to becoming a world church. Will we continue to do so when North American Saints become a minority in the Reorganized Church of Jesus Christ of Latter Day Saints?

Looking to the Future

There is paradox, if not irony, in the future thrust of the RLDS Church. With a basis in ancient Israel and the New Testament church, this particular Latter Day Saint faith community (one of several valid expressions of what Joseph Smith started, by the way) has developed from a separatist movement in rural, nineteenth-century America—more or less outside orthodox Christianity—to become a unique expression of the Christian religion. It offers profound understandings of God's purposes, expressed in one way in North America and, increasingly, in very different ways in the Second and Third Worlds.

It may be that the RLDS Church will find itself in the United States and similar societies primarily addressing other Christian organizations with its peculiar understanding of covenant community. Elsewhere, the church may, instead, infuse existing communities (and often non-Christian ones at that) with RLDS theological understandings. The Temple will function differently in each case, but it will be valid in all of them.

One of the most important functions of the ministries of the Temple for the RLDS Church will be to confirm the reality of God's presence and involvement in the world. This will be made possible through the living sacrifice of Temple workers dedicated to *shalom*, the Hebrew word translated as "peace" but which encompasses a far broader and more active meaning.

That "the temple shall be dedicated to the pursuit of peace" (Doctrine and Covenants 156:5a) implies a holistic approach for the church's ministry: peace within individuals and families, and among persons, groups, and even nations. As the means and facilitator of conflict resolution and enabling—physical, emotional, spiritual, and social—Temple ministries must go far beyond the institutional bounds of the RLDS Church. The Temple, after all, is not *our* house; it is the Lord's. The world community needs such a house. The preparation and practice of Temple ministries—whether in Independence or inner-city Detroit or Papeete or Nairobi—will define the concept of RLDS covenant community as the church enters the twenty-first century. The challenge to "arise and build the Temple" will necessitate looking beyond our past, beyond our own needs and desires, beyond our hierarchical organization, and even beyond a magnificent building so the divine presence, as revealed in the sacrificial nature of Jesus Christ, can find expression in a world that still groans for redemption.

Notes

1. Matthew 27:55; Mark 15:43; Luke 23:46.
2. Jan Shipps, *Mormonism: The Story of a New Religious Tradition* (Urbana and Chicago: University of Illinois Press, 1985).

TEMPLE MINISTRIES CURRICULUM

TEMPLE SCHOOL

TL 100

THE TEMPLE

Lyman F. Edwards

Senior Editor

REORGANIZED CHURCH OF JESUS CHRIST OF LATTER DAY SAINTS

Originally published in the Temple School course ***TL 100, The Temple,*** *Session One, Resource 1.1: 5-15. Used with permission.*

6

A Biblical Background to the Temple Concept

"Look to the heavens and count the stars—if you can," the Lord told Abraham. Then came the promise: "So shall your descendants be." The scriptures record that Abraham "believed the Lord; and he reckoned it to him as righteousness" (Genesis 15:6 RSV). In response to grace, his act of faith brought him into a special relationship with God. He—and his countless heirs—would find blessing in that kind of relationship known as a covenant. Yet Abraham, being human, needed more. He needed a sign or symbol. And in a mysterious and archaic way, that covenant was cut.

The Lord instructed Abraham to bring a heifer, a goat, a ram, a turtledove, and a pigeon. The animals were slaughtered, all except the birds, which were cut in two. When the sun had gone down and Abraham had fallen into a deep sleep, the Lord, hidden in a smoking firepot and flaming torch, passed between the halved carcasses. Thus an ancient ritual was performed. The covenant was put in effect and, as the writer of Genesis attests, a prophecy given foretelling the Exodus and the establishment of a new empire in the Promised Land.

Did Abraham literally have such an experience? Did

he really hear the voice of God telling him what would happen centuries later? Was God truly in the smoke and fire? Our modern penchant for literalism demands an answer. However, the symbolism expressed by this Israelite storyteller is real and true; the divine presence was there somehow, in a way that we can never completely understand. Of course, to speak of God's presence does not explain anything; it merely affirms that God is involved in the midst of human struggle.

Since Abraham's time we human beings have continued to yearn for the gift of being near God. That wonderful experience has occurred in many ways, expressed differently in each culture. Our understandings have come to us particularly through the biblical record kept by Israel, Judaism, and the early Christian Church.

While Abraham's method in seeking divine revelation (cutting up animals) and the way in which God was revealed (a smoking firepot and flaming torch) is remote from our way of thinking, that particular covenant ceremony was familiar to ancients at least as late as the prophet Jeremiah (see Jeremiah 34:18). But therein lies a key to our understanding: Abraham's revelation and his means of seeking it can be understood only within the context of his time and culture.

The Experience of Moses

Centuries later Moses was minding his own business on Mount Horeb one day (actually, he was minding his father-in-law's sheep) when an unusual sight aroused his curiosity: flames and smoke were rising from a bush without it being consumed. What could lay behind this strange occurrence? He investigated, but before he could get close a voice came to him from out of the burning bush: "Take off your shoes, for you are standing on holy ground" (Exodus 3:5 LB). Overcome by awe and probable fright, Moses did as he was commanded.

This was not just a spectacular sight; God was there, hidden within the smoke and fire. Once again in history, the divine presence was manifested—for a reason. God had something for Moses—and only Moses—to do: return to Egypt and lead his Hebrew kinsmen out of slavery.

"Wait just a minute," Moses protested. "How can I do that? I'm just one man—sixty years old at that—and I stutter as well."

The voice came from out of the smoke and fire: "Go to Pharaoh and tell him to 'Let my people go!'"

Moses thought he had discovered a way out of this unpleasant-sounding task by inquiring who it was that would send him. Whose name should he give to Pharaoh? Perhaps who or whatever was behind this voice would be unwilling to part with the knowledge of its name. Ancient people believed there was power in "the name"; there often was reluctance to share it.

The answer to the riddle given to Moses is embedded in an understanding of the ancient Hebrew language, which, partly because it contained no vowels in its written form, adds to its obscurity and difficulty in translation. The best guess of the name is YHWH, which generally has been written Yahweh (pronounced "yawh-way"). Its meaning is, most likely, "That which causes [all things] to be." Our English-language Bibles, however, generally offer a more inadequate translation: "I AM THAT I AM."

In any event, the Deity who summoned Moses to this task was not just another one of the many nature or tribal gods worshiped throughout the Middle East. This was God Most High, the source and sustainer of all creation, who could not be described or known in the usual ways. Hidden within the smoke and fire before Moses was a new revelation, given not just for him to know but for him to respond obediently with a specific act.

What did Moses really experience? What truly took place on that mountainside? What happened beyond a literal understanding of that strange event?

Whatever Moses saw with his naked eye was transformed into a religious sign of the divine presence. His vision awakened him to the realization that he stood on holy ground, for at that mountain rendezvous he was met by God. As in all revelation, normal, ordinary objects and events are understood with sacred meaning by persons who are sensitive to the movement of God. While some religions seek to carry individuals above sensory experience into some sort of total union with Deity, absorbing them like a drop of water in the ocean, this is not typical of Old Testament faith.

Moses' encounter with God sharpened his sense of individuality and made him even more acutely conscious of what God wanted him to do. The voice of God to Moses did not so much come out of a burning bush as it came out of a particular historical situation. There was little if any meaning outside that event, known as the Exodus.

The Mosaic Covenant

Years later Moses returned to those same mountains in the Sinai wilderness, this time as the prophetic leader of the Hebrews, to meet Yahweh. Exodus 19-20 relates that pivotal experience in Israel's history: the giving of the Ten Commandments.

God instructed Moses to gather his people at the foot of the mountain. But only Moses was to climb the mountain while the divine presence descended in a thick cloud upon it. The whole mountain was off limits, so to speak; it became holy ground or "sacred space" because God would be there and nothing profane could tolerate the experience. And so Moses marked out a boundary at the foot of the mountain and went up to meet the Lord. There, in a remarkable vision, Moses received the basis for Israel's faith: "I am the Lord your God, who brought you out of the land of Egypt, out of the house of bondage. You shall have no other gods before me. ..." (Exodus 20:2ff RSV).

The Israelites saw the thick cloud of smoke descend on the mountain, heard the thunder and the blasts of a mighty trumpet, and they were afraid. Only Moses drew near the smokey darkness that hid Yahweh. On behalf of his people, he received the instructions of a new law, which came to be known as the Mosaic Covenant or, simply, the Law. The people learned to whom they belonged, how and why they should offer sacrifice, and numerous rules to govern their special covenant community.

But Yahweh's chosen people were not to remain at the foot of that mountain; many years of desert wandering were ahead before they could enter Canaan. How would the divine presence continue to be revealed? Certainly the cloud-covered mountain could not travel with them! Yahweh provided a way: hovering above and ahead of the Israelite tribes at all times was a spiraling pillar—by day, a cloud of smoke; by night, a flaming fire. The people clearly understood that the pillar, which stretched to heaven, hid Yahweh. When Moses sought divine advice or counsel, the pillar descended in a special place, in a way reminiscent of the dream of Jacob's ladder at Bethel.

That special, movable place was the site of a red-leather tent, known as the Tabernacle or Tent of Meeting (conflicting sources in the Old Testament place it either outside the Israelite encampment or right in its center). There God would come down from heaven to temporarily encamp with them. Later, Israelite writers carefully avoided using the Hebrew word meaning "to dwell" for this event, preferring instead a more archaic word which meant "to tent" or "to tabernacle." They believed that God could not dwell on earth in the same way as human beings; no structure on earth could adequately house or contain the divine presence. But God could visit to bring new revelation through the prophet.

And so Moses would go to the Tent of Meeting and stand in front of it while the cloud which hid Yahweh's presence descended around him. They would "talk," and once the matter had been settled, the cloud would ascend. Moses would return to his people, often with a face that shone so brightly that he would have to cover it for a time.

We know very little of what the Tent of Meeting was actually like. The scriptural accounts date from the time of Solomon's Temple in Jerusalem and therefore are colored by the writers' knowledge of that splendid structure. However, it is quite likely that the Tent served one additional purpose: the resting place of the ark.

This small wooden chest (about four feet long and two-and-a-half feet high and wide, overlayed on top with a large gold plate) was a powerful symbol for the Israelites. It served two distinct functions:

1. ***Receptacle for the Law.*** The tablets containing the Ten Commandments were kept inside the ark and

reminded the people of their covenant relationship with Yahweh established at Mount Sinai. Yahweh had chosen to deposit the Law with them; the ark constantly held before them their responsibilities as a chosen people.

2. **Yahweh's throne**. Because the Israelites were forbidden to form any graven image of Yahweh, it was virtually impossible to fashion a throne for their God. Yet they believed that the divine "mercy seat," as it was called, hovered above the ark and the two statues of cherubim that stood next to it. Cherubim were mythological winged creatures with human heads and animal bodies said to guard the heavenly throne. In Solomon's Temple the cherubim were gold-plated wooden statues; they stretched almost to the ceiling of the divine throne room, the holy of holies. The cherubim in the wilderness Tent of Meeting, no doubt, were much smaller.

Portable Throne of the Invisible God

The ark sometimes is referred to, as well, as the footstool of God. It might seem impossible for the same thing to be both mercy seat and footstool. However, because this was a theological concept rather than a literal object, the Israelites probably had little difficulty dealing with that.

They believed this "portable throne of the invisible God" represented Yahweh's presence in their midst. It traveled at the head of their caravan and went with them into battle to ensure victory (poles were placed through gold rings attached to the side of the ark). Later Israelite writers would even attribute military defeats to the ark's absence.

Both the ark and the Tent of Meeting were sacred. Violators who profaned them by touching the ark or entering the tent were subject to immediate death. These two divine symbols served the Israelites well for their forty years of desert wandering. But once they occupied the Promised Land and began to create a stable, prosperous society, these symbols had to be reinterpreted. Throughout its history Israel struggled with its understanding of the way the presence of Yahweh could "tabernacle" among them. The watershed moment came with King David and the beginning of his royal dynasty.

The tribes of the Hebrew confederacy often lapsed into what might best be called family squabbles. Although there was a central religious shrine at Shechem, where the ark rested in a temporary building and where tribal leaders gathered for festivals to commemorate the Mosaic covenant, the idea of having a king was not universally appealing to tribal patriarchs or prophets.

Their first king, Saul, failed to bring lasting unity; however, his successor, David, achieved greater success. Although David fought many battles and is remembered for numerous achievements, probably his greatest single act was to rescue the ark from obscurity (years before Yahweh had permitted the Philistines to capture it as punishment for Israelite disobedience). With great fanfare King David brought the ark to his capital city, Jerusalem, and placed it in a tent just outside the city walls. This was a bold political and religious move. By doing so he sought to have the divine presence associated in a new way with his royal leadership. He also began plans to build a temple next to his palace but Yahweh's prophet, Nathan, intervened.

Nathan changed his initial approval of the temple idea and publicly prohibited David from proceeding. The reason: David was a man of war whose hands had been stained by the blood of too many battles. If a temple were to be built, it would have to be by a "man of peace." That man would be David's third eldest son, Solomon, whose name had been changed by his father to a derivative of the Hebrew word for peace, *shalom*. (Nathan, through divine revelation, had named him Jedidiah, "beloved of God.") Although David would not be permitted to build a dwelling place for God, Yahweh would establish a house (dynasty) with David, centered in his city of Zion.

A Royal Covenant and Temple

King David began gathering the money and materials necessary for a permanent dwelling place for Yahweh; Solomon made the project his own. He was driven by the fact that Israel's neighbors had erected palaces (temples) for their national gods; Israel should be no different.

The construction of the Temple in Jerusalem, begun in the fourth year of Solomon's reign and completed in the eleventh, was as much a political move as a religious one. The shrewdness of David and Solomon should not be underemphasized in the way they used the unifying religious symbols of the past to mold the tribes into a nation and eventually an empire. Divine approval through the prophets finally was obtained for their ideas; the consent and support of all Israelites was more difficult to acquire. In fact, this may have been the chief reason why the kingdom was divided shortly after Solomon's death.

Solomon's Temple was less a Tent of Meeting than it was a national religious shrine with royal overtones. Standing side by side to Solomon's enormous palace complex, the Temple expressed the theocratic ideal of

Israel: Yahweh had chosen (covenanted with) the Davidic dynasty to rule over the nation. The Temple, then, was the symbol of the Davidic covenant which, in turn, incorporated the ark, the central symbol of the Mosaic covenant. David and Solomon had forged a notable link between their newly created nation-state and the ancient order.

Solomon would want a temple for Yahweh to compete favorably with neighboring temples for other gods. Architects and skilled artisans from throughout the Syrophoenician world were imported to design and furnish the structure. Most of the menial labor was provided by Israelite slaves; burdensome taxes were levied throughout the nation to pay for construction. It should not be surprising, then, that the Temple resembled other temples of that day: a three-roomed, rectangular building with its main entrance on the narrow east end; massive, freestanding bronze pillars at the front door; an elaborate bronze altar in the main chamber with a huge stone altar in the front courtyard; a small, perfect cube at the rear, which served as a divine throne room, set a few feet above the level of the rest of the temple; thick walls employing an intricate pattern of stone and wooden layers; an anteroom for ceremonial washings and the donning of special garments; and a private, side entrance for the king.

Yet Solomon was intent on transforming this somewhat recognizable structure into Yahweh's dwelling place, no doubt believing that Yahweh had taken the initiative in calling him to do so. The issue of providing a permanent abode for God remained a sticky one. This is reflected in the prayer attributed to Solomon at the Temple's dedication: "Will God indeed dwell on the earth? Behold, heaven and the highest heaven cannot contain thee; how much less this house which I have built!" (I Kings 8:27 RSV). Perhaps to appease his critics, Solomon invited Yahweh to allow "his name" to dwell in the Temple.

Of course, the king and more sophisticated Israelites didn't suppose that Yahweh was physically present in the Temple. Nevertheless, the symbolism, borrowed from the wilderness experience but added to considerably, represented a powerful force in Israelite life. The Temple was to be the earthly palace of the heavenly King where, enthroned in the darkness of the inner sanctuary, the holy of holies, Yahweh "dwelt" among the chosen people, ruling and protecting them. The scriptures record that when the Temple was dedicated, a great cloud [of smoke] filled it, driving out all the priests in it at the time.

More Smoke and Fire

The striking imagery of Yahweh hidden within smoke and fire recurs repeatedly. When Isaiah received a vision in the Temple calling him to prophetic service (see Isaiah 6), the sanctuary was filled with smoke, and he envisioned the heavenly throne room. He came to understand that, in spite of all the sacrifices and liturgies in the Temple, the Israelites were still a people of "unclean lips."

Jeremiah, too, preached against a reliance on the outward acts of Temple observance. Standing in the Temple he declared that Yahweh had forsaken his house and abandoned his heritage because the people had broken the covenant made with their ancestors in Sinai. He was very nearly lynched for saying that the Temple should not be viewed as a safe sanctuary to which the people would be protected from all harm. His prophetic ministry highlighted the two opposing ways of viewing Israel's chosenness under God:

1. ***Jeremiah stressed the terms of the Mosaic covenant:*** Yahweh's righteous commandments that no one might disregard with impunity. That wilderness covenant was based on divine grace and contained stipulations to which the nation was obliged to conform. Jeremiah dared to voice the message that his nation could and would be destroyed because it had broken its covenant with Yahweh.

2. ***Jeremiah's opponents stressed the terms of the Davidic covenant:*** Yahweh's sure promises that could not be canceled by anyone or anything. That royal covenant was based on the memory of divine promises to the patriarchs regarding land, posterity, and blessing; this was projected into the future through God's covenant with David. Their voices comforted the people with the message that the nation and dynasty would endure forever because Yahweh had promised it.

Yet the Babylonian conquest ended David's line and, in 587 B.C., left the Temple in total ruin. How would the Israelites respond to the greatest political, social, and religious crisis in their history? Yahweh's symbolic presence, represented by the ark in the Temple, was gone; there was no place to offer acceptable sacrifice; they could no longer look to a divinely appointed king; the chosen people were now captives living in exile.

Somehow, the Israelites kept alive their dream of returning to Zion to rebuild their nation and their religion. They would have to look elsewhere than with the shattered promises of the Davidic covenant, though. Eventually their hopes were fulfilled through the good graces of the Persian emperor, Cyrus, who defeated the Babylonians and began the long process of returning the exiles to Jerusalem, rebuilding the city walls, and paying for a replacement temple. Although not nearly as splendid as Solomon's Temple, the postexilic Temple (often referred to as Zerubbabel's Temple) recreated the same design but with significant changes.

Most of the sacrifices offered in Solomon's Temple had been "communion sacrifices." With these acts, individuals, in concert with the priests, offered thanksgiving for Yahweh's presence and blessings in their lives. This was a covenant celebration, reaffirming their relationship with God. By the time of the divided kingdoms and certainly in Zerubbabel's Temple, however, most individual sacrifice was for expiation (atonement) of sin. No doubt this reflected a more repentant attitude among the Jews who felt a continual need to (1) find grace and (2) ask Yahweh to reestablish the covenant.

Return of the Exiles

Israel returned from exile not as a nation but as a religious community. The holy of holies, what had been considered the divine throne room and the religious center of the nation, was empty as well as dark. But the people still considered it Yahweh's "dwelling place," although this became increasingly more difficult as altars to other gods were erected. Finally, in 167 B.C., the Hellenistic emperor, Antiochus Epiphanes, introduced the worship of Zeus there. For the keepers of the long religious tradition of Israel, this was indeed the "abomination of desolation."

Three years later Judas Maccabee purified and repaired the Temple, built a new altar, and restored worship. Within another century, the Romans became the last in a long line of conquerors to march into Jerusalem. Although Pompey entered the Temple, he respected the sanctuary and did not touch the treasury. In 20-19 B.C. Herod undertook a major Temple rebuilding program, completing it within ten years. Jesus worshiped at Herod's Temple, but its practices and symbolism had changed greatly from the time of Solomon and Moses' wilderness Tent of Meeting.

By Herod's time many Jews had begun to attach cosmic symbolism to the Jerusalem Temple. Influenced by the apocalyptic paganism of Babylon, they placed the Temple in the center of the world, where the Messiah would come to save Israel one last time and bring Yahweh's chosen people to preeminence. Mount Zion (Jerusalem) would be lifted up, symbolically and literally. Since then numerous Christians, including many Latter Day Saints, have attempted to understand the "Temple in Zion" similarly.

There is feeble support for these theories in the Bible. The key to understand the Jerusalem Temple is not in cosmology or apocalypse but in history and the retelling of the story: Liturgical feasts celebrated in the Temple remembered the Exodus; the ark recalled God's covenant with a chosen people; and, by Solomon's time, the Temple signified Yahweh's choice of Jerusalem and David's dynasty.

Herod's Temple was finally destroyed in A.D. 70. Of course, the earliest followers of Jesus, who were all Jews, already had dramatically reduced its significance in their religious life.They believed that the God whose presence had been hidden in the darkness of the holy of holies and in the smoke and fire that symbolized Yahweh back to the time of Abraham was now revealed openly, in the brightness of a new day, in the person of Jesus Christ. This new revelation made a temple building as Israel had understood it irrelevant: "the Word was made flesh and 'tabernacled' [literally, "pitched his tent"] among us"' (John 1:14 JB); the sacrifice of his life made an ultimate atonement; this new covenant established by Christ used imagery and symbolism from the covenants of Abraham, Moses, and David in bringing the possibility of fulfillment to all humankind.

Remembering the Covenant

Covenants, of course, need to be remembered. The earliest Christians remembered the covenant made by God on the day that came to be known as Good Friday. They remembered that as Jesus was nailed to a cross between two common thieves at Golgotha, the Jerusalem garbage dump, the wind began to blow. For them that wind was the "breath of God," which moved at first with gentleness but which soon began to pick up force. As the human life in Jesus drained from his body, the breath of God made its way silently through the twisted alleyways and streets of Jerusalem. At three o'clock, when Jesus died, it had carried angry storm clouds over Jerusalem, and the people there feared the growing darkness and the sound of thunder. Perhaps some of them "remembered" the thunder-filled clouds which settled upon Mount Sinai when Moses made his way up the mountain to covenant with Yahweh.

The wind pushed hard against the outer Temple gates to the Court of the Gentiles, the closest any non-Jew could come to the divine presence. The first of these "Gates of Righteousness" was blown open by a furious burst of wind, followed in turn by those separating the courts of the Israelite women and men. Then the wind, which was the breath of God, rushed past the massive sacrificial altar and broke open the mighty front doors of the Temple. Now swirling with growing force, the wind brought its freshness to the Temple interior where only consecrated priests were permitted. Finally, the veil separating the holy of holies, the throne room of God, from all else began to flutter in the breeze. Then, whipped to a frenzy by the power of God's breath, it tore in two.

On that Good Friday anyone who happened to be near could look in from the profane city, through the gates, into the sacred Temple, and could see what only the High Priest of Israel was permitted to experience each year on the Day of Atonement. There, standing before the awful darkness of Yahweh's presence, he would hold up the sacrificial scapegoat, utter Yahweh's name (an otherwise forbidden act), and sprinkle blood upon the mercy seat and footstool of God in an attempt to cover up the sins of the nation.

But now, at the very moment when Jesus died on a cross at Golgotha, the way was opened for anyone to approach the divine presence. Those earliest Christians remembered that day as the time when God was no longer enthroned in the Temple; henceforth, God's love, power, and presence would be enthroned in the souls of all those who believed on Jesus' name. Their acceptable sacrifices would not be slaughtered animals but their own lives of compassionate, humble service. The torn Temple veil showed that God had "cut a new covenant" and fulfilled the promises to Abraham and his spiritual heirs made in an archaic ceremony centuries before.

This new covenant would have its symbols to help the people remember: baptism by water, confirmation by the laying on of hands, the bread and the cup. The first Christians remembered how Jesus had instructed them to "do this in remembrance of me." His spilled blood, symbolized in the cup, represented the new covenant; his crucified body symbolically replaced the need for animal slaughter on the high altar.

Value for the Twenty-first Century

What can we learn about Israelite and Christian temples that would be of value 2,000 years later? Like the Hellenistic Jews of Jesus' time, we might be tempted to see cosmic significance in another "Temple in Zion." Yet that would be wrong. Solomon's Temple, with its intricate theological mixture of royal covenant and permanent dwelling place of God, is neither appropriate nor helpful either (except, perhaps, for the idea that Christ is "King of Kings"). Certainly, animal sacrifice provides a wrong guide for the twenty-first century.

Perhaps it would be best to draw upon the rich symbolism of the Israelite wilderness experience and its Tent of Meeting. Like the people of Moses, we believe God can be anywhere at anytime, but there is a need for special places—call them sacred space or holy ground or the Temple—for deliberate encounters with Divinity. In that sense, we might gather to the center of our faith community to tabernacle with God for a while. That sacred experience would then challenge us to go back to more "profane" territory, representing Jesus Christ through sacrificial service as the body of Christ.

The ancient Israelites understood the idea of Yahweh coming down from heaven and humankind reaching up from earth in the symbol of a spiraling pillar of smoke and fire. Israel's past was always with them, symbolized in the tablets of the Mosaic covenant contained in the ark. Those same concepts can now be symbolically understood in a new way in the magnificent spiral design of the Temple itself, which carries its beginning point with it, yet continually moves outward and upward.

As the spiritual descendants of Abraham, Moses, David, and Jesus, we live in a unique covenant relationship with God. God is not hidden from us in smoke and fire as in Israel's experience but is revealed in the person of Jesus Christ, whose new covenant gives our lives meaning—as individuals and as a community. The Temple shall stand, then, as an architectural symbol of that community—the body of Christ.

TEMPLE MINISTRIES CURRICULUM

TEMPLE SCHOOL

TL 100

THE TEMPLE

Lyman F. Edwards

Senior Editor

REORGANIZED CHURCH OF JESUS CHRIST OF LATTER DAY SAINTS

Originally published in the Temple School course, ***TL 100, The Temple,*** *Session One, Resource 1.2: 16-21. Used with permission.*

7

A Restoration Perspective on the Temple Concept

St. Francis once was asked what his response would be if, by revelation, he knew the Savior would return the following day. His reported reply: "First thing, I'd finish hoeing this row." The story of the Restoration movement follows a people intent to "finish hoeing the row" in anticipation of the coming kingdom of God.

This unique, "peculiar" religious movement began in 1820 with an adolescent boy concerned with his own sinfulness in a world that seemed—at least to him—unadorned by the "holy walk and Godly conversation" he found described in scripture. A decade after his remarkable experience, commonly referred to today as the First Vision, Joseph Smith, Jr., attempted to put this mystical event into words. His description included the following [original spellings retained]:

> I cried unto the Lord for mercy for there was none else to whom I could go... and the Lord heard my cry in the wilderness and while in the attitude of calling upon the Lord in the 16th year of my age a piller of ~~fire~~ light above the brightness of the Sun at noon day come down from above and rested upon me and I was filled with the Spirit of God and the Lord opened the heavens upon me and

> I saw the Lord and he spake unto me saying Joseph my son thy Sins are forgiven thee. go thy way walk in my statutes and keep my commandments behold I am the Lord of glory I was crucifyed for the world that all those who believe on my name may have Eternal life.... .and lo I come quickly as it was written of me in the cloud clothed in the Glory of my Father and my soul was filled with love and for many days I could rejoice with great joy and the Lord was with me but could find none that would believe the heavnly vision... [1]

The experience of the First Vision was remarkable for Joseph and has become important since then for the many branches of the religious movement he founded. It is easy to forget the First Vision was not generally known until the Nauvoo era. The account of the First Vision most commonly remembered today was not prepared by Joseph until 1842 for publication in the church newspaper, *Times and Seasons*, and depicts a rather different and more complex experience. The later version probably reflects the eventful history of Joseph's persecuted band of Saints and perhaps should be understood within that context.

If the First Vision did not provide the impetus for the remarkable growth of the church in its first decade, what did? Certainly part of the answer is the unusual, new book of scripture brought to light by Joseph Smith—the Book of Mormon. In the stories of several "lost tribes of Israel," the Book of Mormon expanded the scope of divine revelation: Jesus Christ is the Savior of the New World as well as the Old. However, there had to be more to it than that, because the Bible (particularly the New Testament) still provided the basic missionary text during those early years. Perhaps what attracted tens of thousands of Americans to the church was a "living prophet" who envisioned a new order, a New Jerusalem—

Zion—out on the frontier, with a temple at its center. Such vision meshed and updated two ancient theological concepts: righteous city and temple.

Although the Saints had begun to gather in increasing numbers from western New York and Pennsylvania to Kirtland, Ohio, within a few months of the church's founding, that location would not provide the site for the city of Zion. The Saints' land of inheritance, Joseph prophesied, was on the far frontier: the rough, bustling town of Independence, Missouri. Visiting there in July 1831, Joseph produced a revelation addressed to the elders accompanying him on the trip.

> Wherefore this is the land of promise, and the place for the city of Zion. ... Behold, the place which is now called Independence, is the Center Place, and the spot for the temple is lying westward upon a lot which is not far from the courthouse; wherefore it is wisdom that the land should be purchased by the Saints; and also every tract lying westward, even unto the line running directly between Jew and Gentile. And also every tract bordering by the prairies, inasmuch as my disciples are enabled to buy lands. Behold, this is wisdom, that they may obtain it for an everlasting inheritance.
>
> —Doctrine and Covenants 57:1

By the end of that month the sixty members of the Colesville, New York, Branch had relocated from temporary quarters near Kirtland to settle in Jackson County, about twelve miles west of Independence. Within two years about 1,200 Saints had "gathered to Zion." But before ending his first visit to the city of Zion in August 1831, Joseph spoke through revelation emphasizing the importance of the task:

> I give unto my servant Sidney Rigdon a commandment that he shall write a description of the land of Zion, and a statement of the will of God, as it shall be made known

> by the Spirit, unto him; and an epistle and subscription, to be presented unto all the churches, to obtain moneys, to be put into the hands of the bishop, to purchase lands for an inheritance for the children of God.....The Lord willeth that the disciples, and the children of men, should open their hearts even to purchase this whole region of country, as soon as time will permit...and let the work of the gathering be not in haste, nor by flight, but let it be done as it shall be counseled by the elders of the church at the conferences, according to the knowledge which they receive from time to time. And let my servant Sidney Rigdon consecrate and dedicate this land, and the spot of the temple, unto the Lord.
>
> —Doctrine and Covenants 58:11-13

Two days later, on August 3, 1831, according to Oliver Cowdery's eyewitness account preserved in John Whitmer's history, eight elders (Joseph Smith, Oliver Cowdery, Sidney Rigdon, Peter Whitmer, Jr., Frederick G. Williams, W. W. Phelps, Martin Harris, and Joseph Coe)

> ...assembled together where the temple is to be erected. Sidney Rigdon dedicated the ground where the city is to stand, and Joseph Smith, Junior, laid a stone at the northeast corner of the contemplated temple in the name of the Lord Jesus of Nazareth. After all present had rendered thanks to the Great Ruler of the universe, Sidney Rigdon pronounced this spot of ground wholly dedicated unto the Lord for ever. Amen.[2]

By mid-December Bishop Edward Partridge had purchased a sixty-three-acre tract from Jones H. Flournoy that historically has come to be known as the temple lot. The temple site dedicated in August was within that tract, although its exact location has never been precisely identified. (For a detailed examination of this point, see "The Spot for the Temple" by Richard P. Howard, church historian, in the June 1987 *Saints Herald*.)

In September 1832 Joseph presented a revelation combining Old Testament concepts with the Church of Christ: "the city New Jerusalem shall be built ... beginning at this place, even the place of the temple ... and a cloud shall rest upon it, which cloud shall be even the glory of the Lord" (Doctrine and Covenants 83:2a-b).

Joseph's prophetic discernment and imagination constantly were being stretched and refined. Although a site for the temple in Zion had been determined, its form and functions were never realized beyond the level of general guidelines and rough architectural sketches. Mob violence drove the Saints from Jackson County in late 1833. Although they continued to build up Kirtland (where a "House of the Lord" was built) and established other communities in northern Missouri before centering church activity in Nauvoo, Illinois, the Saints never gave up their dream of the temple in the city of Zion.

An important part of Joseph's temple concept was the founding of a School of the Prophets in Kirtland and a proposed School of the Elders in Zion. In this regard he presented prophetic direction to the church:

> Seek ye diligently and teach one another words of wisdom; yea, seek ye out of the best books words of wisdom; seek learning even by study, and also by faith. Organize yourselves; prepare every needful thing, and establish a house, even a house of prayer, a house of fasting, a house of faith, a house of learning, a house of glory, a house of order, a house of God.
>
> —Doctrine and Covenants 85:36a-b

The Kirtland Temple (as it came to be known during the early years of the Reorganization) was built in response to this pattern. The sacrificial activity of the Kirtland Saints led to an outpouring of spiritual manifestations (divine presence) during the dedication services in spring 1836. Yet that structure has always functioned more as a meetinghouse and tourist site rather than a temple, despite the popular usage of its name. A similar structure contemplated for Independence—one of twenty-four buildings envisioned for temple functions—was never built, of course. More importantly, a city of Zion, which would have required a temple at its center, was never built either. Those twin concepts could have been realized only together.

Some of the Saints who gathered in Far West, Missouri, made a start on temple building in the middle of their fledgling city. Temple building in Nauvoo provides a different story entirely.

Rising from the high bluff overlooking a bend in the Mississippi River, the Nauvoo Temple represented—in symbolic and literal ways—the center of that unique faith community. The Saints had been through a great deal in just one decade: persecution, migration, rapid expansion, and a tremendous theological/religious development. Their prophet, Joseph Smith, had come a long way from being the troubled teenager, preoccupied by personal shortcomings. With some 30,000 followers he now provided theological, organizational, civil, military, and economic leadership. Nauvoo, the "City Beautiful," was his city and reflected his qualities: complex, growing, and constantly changing. But the church had become more than any one person—even this one—could control.

Forces at work inside the church and outside in "gentile" society created mounting tensions. Theological speculation by Joseph and other top church leaders, particularly concerning the afterlife, had led to the introduction of new doctrines and practices. These were reflected in the Nauvoo Temple. Proxy baptisms for the dead were performed in the basement by November 1841. Within months of Joseph and Hyrum's death in June 1844, an elaborate endowment ritual, which included strong Masonic overtones, began to be performed for "worthy" Saints. Indeed, the pattern for later temple building and practice in Utah had its formation in Nauvoo. However, the theological expression of city and temple in Nauvoo was rejected by the Saints who formed the Reorganization as incompatible with their interpretation of the Restoration movement. While the Kirtland example of temple building can offer us some insights today in the way that a "House of the Lord" can function at the center of a Restoration faith community, the Nauvoo example provides little if anything at all.

During the first century of the Reorganization, the church dealt with its uniqueness as a covenant community within an evermore pluralistic Christian community and secular world. The church concerned itself with a host of issues: a new gathering; democracy and autocracy within a theocratic order; the role of presidency; the functioning of priesthood, especially the role of bishops. Additionally, the church had been too busy being "not Mormon" to spend time, effort, or money on a dream of the Temple.

Perhaps it has been fortunate that the Reorganization could not have afforded a temple until now; it has taken us a long time to catch up our theological understandings of one. It has been only in recent decades that we have begun to see ourselves in more than historical terms and have adopted an incarnational approach—how God, in Christ, is "in us." This challenges us to change our emphasis from authority to divine calling, from light to leaven in society, and from end result to process. As Paul M. Edwards stated, "We have used our history as a theology," and thus in some ways have been slow to claim the distinct values of each.[3]

Almost a century and a half after Joseph Smith, Jr., called for a temple in the city of Zion, another prophet reissued the challenge. Yet this new temple in Zion would be built in the "Center Place" of a very different faith community, located in a radically changed world. In 1984, sixteen years after his father, W. Wallace Smith, issued a call to begin preparations, President Wallace B. Smith presented an inspired document to the World Conference that included the following:

> The temple shall be dedicated to the pursuit of peace. It shall be for reconciliation and for healing of the spirit. It shall also be for a strengthening of faith and preparation for witness. By its ministries an attitude of body, mind, and spirit as a desirable end toward which to strive will be fostered. It shall be the means for providing leadership education for priesthood and member. And it shall be a place in which the essential meaning of the Restoration as healing and redeeming agent is given new life and understanding, inspired by the life and witness of the Redeemer of the world.
>
> —Doctrine and Covenants 156:5

There are many forces that could easily sidetrack us from understanding the Temple. Like the thousands of Christians in Joseph Smith's day who expected an immediate return of Jesus (a view common among Latter Day Saints as well), we might be tempted to tie the Temple to expectations regarding "end times." Yet that would be as inappropriate for us as it was for the Hellenistic Jews of Jesus' day. We might also be influenced by other Latter Day Saint temples, including the one in Nauvoo. But that would be just as inappropriate, for they represent a different direction for the Restoration movement from what the Reorganization chose from its beginning. The Nauvoo pattern—elaborated in Utah—is recognizably different from our present understandings of God's presence and activity in the world, especially our belief in Jesus Christ.

The Temple can be a powerful symbol. It can remind us of a teenage boy who sought divine help in dealing with his personal sinfulness and shortcomings and who, as a result, was confronted by a vision of Christ in a spiraling pillar of light; as a result he was forgiven and cleansed. Joseph Smith later went on to lead a people out on the frontier seeking to build a city of God with a temple at its center. Today we are called by God to move out on a different kind of frontier.

Our past, our present, and our future find direction and purpose in this new symbol—the Temple. It can be understood in many ways: through the experiences of our ancestors; the struggles and journeys of Restoration Saints; the understandings of those from other cultures who are no longer "strangers and foreigners" to us because of Christ Jesus; and in the challenges of our own time. Although Joseph Smith, Jr., first issued the call to build, the Temple in the Center Place of Zion is *ours*; more importantly, it is God's. It becomes, then, both a gift of grace and a response of faith.

Notes

1. Quoted in Richard P. Howard, "An Analysis of Six Contemporary Accounts Touching Joseph Smith's First Vision," in Maurice L. Draper and Clare D. Vlahos, eds., *Restoration Studies I* (Independence, Missouri: Herald Publishing House, 1980): 97.
2. Quoted in John Whitmer, "The book of John Whitmer. Kept by Commandment," as published in F. Mark McKiernan and Roger D. Launius, eds., *An Early Latter Day Saint History* (Independence, Missouri: Herald Publishing House, 1980), 32.
3. Paul M. Edwards, "The Secular Smiths," in Maurice L. Draper and A. Bruce Lindgren, eds., *Restoration Studies II* (Independence, Missouri: Herald Publishing House, 1983): 96.

Originally published in ***Studies in the Doctrine & Covenants, Volume 3*** *(Independence, Missouri: Herald Publishing House, 1989), 9-13.*

8

An Ensign of Grace and Faith

Let the work of planning go forward, and let the resources be gathered in, that the building of my temple may be an ensign to the world of the breadth and depth of the devotion of the Saints. —Doctrine and Covenants 156:6

My invitation to come and be received is being extended even now so that the blessings of fellowship and participation in the body may be enjoyed once more. Come and be reconciled in my body is the healing word to those who are saddened and downhearted. In the many places where you are called to labor, the forces of darkness and destruction are active indeed, and seem to hold sway. Your hearts are burdened by the magnitude of the tasks that are yours in bringing the light of my gospel into such darkness. Nevertheless, I have heard your prayers when you have cried out to me, and I have been with you in the places where you occupy. I am aware of your desires to serve me and my assurance is that as you go forth, your offerings of faith and service are acceptable to me. In all your efforts, therefore, continue to

trust in my grace and respond in love to the leadings of my Spirit. If you will come before me in unity and love I will bless you with a great outpouring of compassion, both for one another and for the world into which you are sent. Amen. —Doctrine and Covenants 157:15-17

One of the more memorable scenes in the classic 1969 movie, *The Graduate*, has the character portrayed by Dustin Hoffman attending a party in honor of his college graduation. One of his parents' friends corners him to share a piece of advice which this man feels is the one—perhaps only—thing that the new graduate needs to know to succeed in life. After a dramatic pause, the word rolls off the man's tongue: Plastics! Yes, that will provide the key to the future; fame and fortune will belong to whoever masters plastics. The graduate, however, is less than enthusiastic about basing his future on that, feeling there must be more to life. Most of us would agree.

Of course, there is always a danger in trying to reduce anything, especially something like the "key to the future" or the "meaning and purpose of life," to a single word or concept. But in establishing a starting point, it can make an interesting exercise. Asked to identify *the* key to understanding the Temple, I might be tempted to choose a real mouthful of a term: *deoxyribonucleic acid*. Fortunately, it has a shorter name—DNA.

Anyone with a moderate interest in science knows that the DNA molecule is the basic building block of life. Without its twenty-three pairs of chromosomes, there can be no life forms, just dead matter. Viewed under a powerful microscope, the twin-helix spiral of the DNA molecule can be seen wherever living organisms exist.

It is the one component shared by everyone alive. How appropriate, then, that the spiral form, found in the DNA twin-helix and in so many other ways throughout nature, provides the basic shape for the Temple's architectural design. Of all the spirals found in nature, perhaps the DNA twin-helix spiral can offer us the deepest symbolic meaning.

President Wallace B. Smith has noted the importance of the spiral form for the Temple design.

> It has been described as the curve of life—an expression of natural strength and energy....The spiral form has a single-point source of origin and emanates outward, expanding infinitely without deviating in form....[It] retains its shape as it grows in one dimension by adding substance at the open end. There is no such thing as a *static* spiral. And this makes a wonderful symbol for the church.... Examining the spiral design reveals that the source is not discovered by finding the center, as in a circle or sphere, or by dissecting its sides as in a square or triangle. Rather, the source is revealed by actively participating in its movement, following the design back to its origin or forward toward infinity.[1]

It is significant that the design comes from nature for a number of reasons. Perhaps the most important has been outlined by Rod Downing who wrote in the *Saints Herald* that

> our well-being is caught up in the well-being of the whole planetary biosphere. For me, the Temple design symbolizes the integration of peace with nature, with the well-being of all life. But it must be more than symbol: It must become a very real leavening and transforming influence through its programs and projects; otherwise, it is just an empty shell.[2]

Twin Theological Strands

As there are twin strands in the DNA helix, so too are there "twin theological strands" represented in the Temple spiral. As a symbol of who we belong to and what we are called to be and do as a community, the Temple is both a gift of God's grace and a response of our faith. It will stand as beautiful evidence to the world of "a shining symbol of [God's] love" (Doctrine and Covenants 157:8). Likewise, the building of the Temple will be "an ensign to the world of the breadth and depth of the devotion of the Saints" (Doctrine and Covenants 156:6).

For centuries Christians have engaged in a "grace versus works" debate. And some people have mistakenly equated "works" with faith. But faith is most deeply understood as a divine gift. In that sense, it becomes inappropriate and unfortunate to view grace and faith as representing opposite extremes. After all, the essence of the Restoration movement is a marvelous blending of both. The Saints have always considered that their faith involves more than mental assent or their own actions. In fact, their expression of faith comes close to the Apostle Paul's original meaning for the Greek term, *pistis Jesu Christou* (the "faith—or more accurately, faithfulness—of Jesus Christ"), which he develops especially in Galatians and Romans as an understanding of what is necessary for salvation.

> But now the righteousness of God without the law is manifested, being witnessed by the law and the prophets; even the righteousness of God which is by faith [*pistis*] of Jesus Christ unto all and upon all them that believe; for there is no difference; for all have sinned, and come short of the glory of God; therefore being justified only by his grace through the redemption that is in Christ Jesus; whom God has set forth to be a

> propitiation through faith in his blood, to declare his righteousness for the remission of sins that are past, through the forbearance of God.... Therefore we conclude that a [person] is justified by faith alone without the deeds of the law. —Romans 3:21-25, 28

Paul's use of the Greek word *pistis* is usually translated as "faith." But his meaning implies far more than merely trust or an activity of the mind and includes the "believing obedience" made possible by God's intervention or assistance. It is interesting also that Joseph Smith, Jr., maintained the use of the term "faith *of* Jesus Christ" found in the Authorized (King James) Version when he produced his translation (commonly referred to today as the Inspired Version or IV). Many modern translations have changed this phrase to read "faith *in* Jesus Christ," perhaps because that interpretation is more satisfactory theologically to many Christians. However, a study of the Greek grammar in the oldest available texts supports the KJV and IV usage. Paul is saying, then, that it is the *pistis* or faithfulness of Jesus Christ (a divine act) that brings justification to humankind, thus opening the door to the possibility of salvation. Because we have all sinned and have fallen short of the glory of God, our only hope for the future comes by grace.

Abundant Grace Is Free

God's grace is given freely and in abundance; there is no absolute command to *do* anything in response. This question could well be asked then: What will happen *if* we do nothing after experiencing grace? *Nothing*. Yet if we wish to accept God's invitation to be involved in the great task of bringing forth the kingdom of God on earth—the cause of Zion—*then* there is an implied responsibility. This is reflected in the prophetic direction given to the church in 1964 through W. Wallace Smith: "Stewardship is the response of my people to the ministry of my Son and is required alike of all those who seek to build the kingdom" (Doctrine and Covenants 147:5a). The concept and symbol of the Temple is, perhaps, the ultimate architectural expression of this understanding.

We are *apprehended* by divine grace; it is not something we are able to find or acquire on our own. As Paul Tillich has written,*

> We cannot transform our lives, unless we allow them to be transformed by that stroke of grace....Grace strikes us when we are in great pain and restlessness. It strikes us when we walk through the dark valley of a meaningless and empty life. It strikes us when we feel that our separation is deeper than usual, because we have violated another life, a life which we loved, or from which we were estranged. It strikes us when our disgust for our own being, our indifference, our weakness, our hostility, and our lack of direction and composure have become intolerable to us. It strikes us when, year after year, the longed-for perfection of life does not appear, when the old compulsions reign within us as they have for decades, when despair destroys all joy and courage. Sometimes at that moment a wave of light breaks into our darkness, and it is as though a voice were saying: "You are accepted. *You are accepted*, accepted by that which is greater than you, and the name of which you do not know. Do not ask for the name now; perhaps you

---

> will find it later. Do not seek for anything; do not perform anything; do not intend anything. *Simply accept the fact that you are accepted!*" If that happens to us, we experience grace. After such an experience we may not be better than before, and we may not believe more than before. But everything is transformed. In that moment, grace conquers sin, and reconciliation bridges the gulf of estrangement. And nothing is demanded of this experience, no religious or moral or intellectual presupposition, nothing but *acceptance*.[3]

The life and ministry of Jesus provides the fullest expression of God's grace known to humankind. Jesus sought to reconcile human beings to one another and their creator, to bring light where there had been only darkness, to replace brokenness and disease with wholeness and perfect health. It is no coincidence, then, that the call for the church to "arise and build the Temple" comes at a time of great discord and dissention, when "the forces of darkness and destruction are active indeed, and seem to hold sway" (Doctrine and Covenants 157:16a). And so a prophetic word has come to the church to bring an assurance of grace:

> I have heard your prayers when you have cried out to me, and I have been with you in places where you occupy. I am aware of your desires to serve me and my assurance is that as you go forth, your offerings of faith and service are acceptable to me. In all your efforts, therefore, continue to trust in my grace and respond in love to the leadings of my Spirit.
>
> —Doctrine and Covenants 157:16b-17

Encountering Christ

The promise is given to the church that God's blessings will include "a great outpouring of compassion, both for one another and for the world into which you are sent" (Doctrine and Covenants 157:17). This suggests that our understanding of the world will be transformed as we "encounter" Jesus Christ in the Temple, perhaps in ways as significant as the transformed life of Saul of Tarsus who met the risen Christ on the road to Damascus as the first step in becoming Paul, Christ's "apostle to the Gentiles."

The changes that occurred in Paul's life were not so much from bad to good in a moral sense (see Philippians 3:6) or a conversion from one religion to another—he did not, after all, stop being a Jew when he became a Christian. Rather, he saw God's plan of salvation in a totally new light to include, *by grace*, all of humankind and not just the narrow confines of Judaism. The Temple, then, with its spirit of inclusiveness shall cast new light on our world and shall be a symbol of reconciliation and healing. Our individual lives and the role of the church in the world can find new meaning and purpose. The experience of grace offers the chance—*and the risk*—of a new way of life. The fact that grace comes first and never as a result of our human endeavoring is illustrated by an old story from India.[4] It seems that every day, just outside a small village, an old man sat cross-legged mixing dirt with water in an old pot. After hours of stirring he would reach into the pot and pull out a large gold nugget. Every day people watched him, waiting for the moment when he would reach into the muddy water for the gold nugget, then express their absolute amazement.

One day a young man came by and asked, "Please show me how you do your magic." The old man kindly offered to do so.

"It is not difficult," he said. "It requires only that I pour common dirt and water in an ordinary pot and stir it with a simple stick. After I stir it awhile a lump of gold forms, and I reach in to remove it."

The young man eagerly undertook to follow the old man's directions. He stirred dirt and water together into an old pot all day long, stopping frequently to see if the gold had begun to form. He continued on into the next day, even well after dark. But despite all his effort, no gold nuggets appeared—not even a tiny one. Finally, he went back for further instructions.

The old man politely asked him to repeat what he had been doing, step by step, and so the young man recounted everything he had done. The old man thought for a moment, then said, "It seems I neglected to include one important detail. While you stir you must *never* think about the gold."

Once the experience of grace has come and its recipient has decided to respond to God's offer to assist in bringing to fruition the great peaceable era foreseen by prophets for centuries, there is still no guarantee of a new order or "city" progressing in a methodical manner toward ultimate goodness. Such a New Jerusalem doesn't necessarily *have to* happen—but it *can*. Speaking from a more or less "secular" perspective, Alvin Toffler foresees the establishment of a new society which he terms a "practopia"—neither a grand utopia filled with beauty and goodness nor a grim, faceless society such as found in *1984* or *Brave New World*. It is, instead

> neither the best nor the worst of all possible worlds, but one that is both practical and preferable to the one we had. Unlike a utopia, a practopia is not free of disease, political nastiness, and bad manners. Unlike most utopias, it is not static or frozen in unreal perfection. Nor is it reversionary, modeling itself on some imagined ideal of the past.[5]

Conversely, Toffler maintains, a practopia does not embody the "crystallized evil of a utopia turned inside out." It is neither ruthlessly antidemocratic nor inherently militarist, and its citizens are not reduced to faceless uniformity. Likewise, a practopia does not destroy its neighbors or degrade its environment. In short, a practopia offers a positive and revolutionary alternative, yet it is realistically attainable. "One can glimpse in it a civilization that makes allowance for individual difference, and embraces (rather than suppresses) racial, regional, religious, and subcultural variety."[6]

The Gathering

Traditionally, one of the clearest expressions of the Saints' faith response has been the idea of the "gathering." We have longed to come—or even *flee*—to Zion. This has been understood usually as a literal, physical gathering. But a far deeper meaning may come as we extend our ideas of the gathering from methods based on transportation to those involving communication. Within the past few years, methods of "traveling" by means of satellite telecommunication have made it possible for groups of people thousands of miles apart to experience an event *together* with relative ease and at a cost far less than transporting them by conventional means over land, sea, and air. Previous generations who dreamed of gathering to Zion could not have even imagined this possibility. Yet for us, today, it is relatively commonplace. What was the *only* way to gather a century and a half ago has been superseded since.

The gathering, the city of Zion, the Temple, the Second Coming, the Endowment—these are all terms that have been understood in various ways at different times in our history. Undoubtedly, they will continue to undergo reinterpretation and transformation. Of course, there is probably a natural human tendency to want to establish *one right way*, and this has been true within the Restoration movement at times as well. It may be helpful in arriving at our own understandings to look at the story of "The Magic Ring," adapted from a tale attributed to Moses Mendelssohn, one of the eighteenth century's most brilliant thinkers.[7]

A woman once asked her teacher, "Which is the true religion?" The teacher replied as follows: Once there was a magic ring which gave its bearer the gifts of grace, kindness, and generosity. When the owner of the ring was on his deathbed, his three sons came separately and asked him for the ring. The old man promised the ring to each of them.

He then sent for the finest jeweler in the kingdom and paid him to make two rings identical to the original. The jeweler did so, and before he died, the father gave each son a ring without telling him about the other two. Inevitably, the three sons discovered that each one had a ring, and they appeared before the local judge to ask his help in deciding who had the magic one.

The judge examined the rings but found them all to be alike. He then said, "Why must anyone decide now? We shall know who has the magic ring when we observe the direction your life takes." From that time on each of the brothers acted as if he had the magic ring by being kind, honest, and thoughtful.

"Now," the teacher concluded, "religions are like the three brothers in the story. The moment their members cease striving for justice and love we will know their religion is not the one God gave the world."

Looking Ahead

We will always be tempted to see the Temple as a symbol of God's grace offered to *us*; likewise, we could understand the Temple merely as *our* response of faith. And while it is indeed true that *our* past, present, and future find direction and purpose in this new "shining symbol," it can—and perhaps *must*— be understood in many more ways. The experiences of our forebears dating back to Old Testament times, the struggles and journeys of Restoration Saints, the understandings of people from other cultures who are no longer "strangers and foreigners" because of Jesus Christ, and the challenges of our own time call us to "look beyond." For even though Joseph Smith, Jr., first issued the call to build, the Temple in the Center Place of Zion is not just *ours*, it is God's and therefore belongs to God's people throughout the whole, wide world. It is *their* ensign of grace and faith as well as our own.

The words of a new hymn by Barbara and Richard Howard give great meaning to this symbolic understanding of the Temple. "Come Be Reconciled, My People" can be sung to the tune, "Hyfrydol" (*Hymns of the Saints* 17).

Come be reconciled, my people,
In my body you are healed.
I am with you is my promise,
In my love am I revealed.
Let my Spirit gently lead you,
Let my mercy all embrace;
To a world that yearns for freedom,
Give compassion; trust my grace.

May the Temple rise in beauty—
Shining symbol of my love.

To a world of war and anguish
May my peace come as a dove.
Let my Spirit move among you
Freeing you from hate and fear,
Healing wounds with love's anointing,
Bringing peace and justice near.

Notes

1. Wallace B. Smith, "Inspiring Times for Temple Planners," *Saints Herald* Vol. 135, No. 10 (October 1988):19-20.
2. Rod Downing, "Peace and Our Ecological Survival," *Saints Herald* Vol.. 136, No. 5 (May 1989): 11.
3. Paul Tillich, excerpted from "You Are Accepted" in *The Shaking of the Foundations*. Copyright 1948 Charles Scribner's Sons; copyright renewed 1976, Hannah Tillich. Used with permission.
4. Adapted from a story quoted by William R. White, *Stories for the Journey: A Sourcebook for Christian Storytellers* (Minneapolis, Minnesota: Augsburg Publishing House, 1988), 100-101.
5. Alvin Toffler, *The Third Wave* (New York: William Morrow/Bantam Books Inc., 1981), 357-358.
6. Ibid.
7. Adapted from *Stories for the Journey*, 54-55.

Originally published in ***Studies in the Doctrine & Covenants, Volume 3*** *(Independence, Missouri: Herald Publishing House, 1989), 19-23.*

9

The Temple and the Body of Christ

My servants have been diligent in the work of planning for the building of my temple in the Center Place. Let this work continue at an accelerated rate, according to the instructions already given, for there is great need of the spiritual awakening that will be engendered by the ministries experienced within its walls. Indeed, these ministries shall be the means of great blessing for you, my people, if you will heed the counsel of my servants of the First Presidency who are rightly charged with the responsibility of developing the specific details of these ministries.

The priesthood offices already provided for in my church have always had the potential of supplying these blessings. Some of their functions, however, will be expanded and given additional meaning as the purposes of temple ministries are revealed more fully.... Hear, O my people, regarding my holy priesthood. The power of this priesthood was placed in your midst from the earliest days of the rise of this work for the blessing and salvation of humanity.... It is my will that my priesthood be made

up of those who have an abiding faith and desire to serve me with all their hearts, in humility and with great devotion....

I have heard the prayers of many, including my servant the prophet, as they have sought to know my will in regard to the question of who shall be called to share the burdens and responsibilities of priesthood in my church. I say to you now, as I have said in the past, that all are called according to the gifts which have been given them. This applies to priesthood as well as to any other aspects of the work. Therefore, do not wonder that some women of the church are being called to priesthood responsibilities. This is in harmony with my will and where these calls are made known to my servants, they may be processed according to administrative procedures and provisions of the law....
—Doctrine and Covenants 156:3-4, 7a, 8a, 9a-c

The story is told of Moses Mendelssohn, who is remembered today, two centuries later, as a brilliant scholar. When it was time for him to marry, his father made the customary arrangements for him to wed. Although a poor scribe, Moses' father managed somehow to get the father of Fromet Guggenheim—a beautiful and wealthy young woman—to agree to marry his son. Although a compassionate and sensitive young man, Moses Mendelssohn was neither wealthy nor good-looking. In fact, he was short, quite ugly, and a hunchback.

A party was arranged so the two could meet for the first time. Before they could be introduced, however, Fromet Guggenheim saw him from a distance and was immediately repulsed. In no uncertain terms she told her father the engagement was off.

When Moses was advised of her demand, he asked to speak with her alone. After chatting quietly for a few minutes, he said, "I wish to tell you a story."

"As you know," he began, "all marriages are arranged in heaven. Before I was born an angel was escorting me to earth, and I asked if it was possible for me to see the woman God had selected for me. The angel answered that though that was unusual, it was not an impossible request.

"I was granted one look, and to my astonishment the woman had an ugly hump on her back. I pleaded with God, 'It is not fair that a woman be a hunchback. She will be the object of scorn and contempt. I beg you, give me the hump and let her be well formed and beautiful.' "

Moses Mendelssohn was silent a moment before he concluded. "God heard my prayer and granted my wish. I am that boy and you are that girl."

Fromet Guggenheim now looked at Moses Mendelssohn with different eyes. The man she saw—and later married—was not a short, ugly hunchback but a wonderfully "attractive" man filled with warmth and compassion.[1]

There are many questions we might ask to connect this story with the emerging understanding of the Temple. For example, how might it relate to the admonition in Doctrine and Covenants 150:10b to "bear the burden of their sin"? As well, there would be profit in relating Moses Mendelssohn's example to Doctrine and Covenants 157:17. "If you will come before me in unity and love I will bless you with a great outpouring of compassion, both for one another and for the world into which you are sent." What was his key to successfully persuading the young woman to marry him and how could that help us discover a pattern for Temple ministry?

Keys of the Kingdom

The Restoration movement has placed great emphasis on the idea of "keys" in regard to both priesthood roles and the kingdom of God. Keys, of course, provide the power to unlock doors for those who are given the authority to do so. Here are only a few of the many references in the Doctrine and Covenants.

> The keys of the kingdom of God are committed unto man on the earth, and from thence shall the gospel roll forth unto the ends of the earth, as the stone which is cut out of the mountain without hands shall roll forth, until it has filled the whole earth.
>
> —Doctrine and Covenants 65:1b

> It is my will that an house should be built unto me in the land of Zion...for a place of thanksgiving, for all Saints, and for a place of instruction for all those who are called to the work of the ministry, in all their several callings, and offices; that they may be perfected in the understanding of their ministry; in theory; in principle and in doctrine; in all things pertaining to the kingdom of God on the earth, the keys of which kingdom have been conferred upon you.
>
> —Doctrine and Covenants 94:3

> The power and authority of the higher, or Melchisedec, priesthood, is to hold the keys of all the spiritual blessings of the church; to have the privilege of receiving the mysteries of the kingdom of heaven; to have the heavens opened unto them; to commune with the general assembly and church of the Firstborn; and to enjoy the communion and presence of God the Father, and Jesus the Mediator of the new covenant.
>
> —Doctrine and Covenants 104:9

The power and authority of the lesser, or Aaronic, priesthood is, to hold the keys of the ministering of angels, and to administer in outward ordinances—the letter of the gospel—the baptism of repentance for the remission of sins, agreeably to the covenants and commandments. —Doctrine and Covenants 104:10

Matthew's Gospel provides the account of Jesus conferring keys on Peter; John's Gospel extends this to all of the Twelve as a commission from the risen Christ.

And I will give unto thee the keys of the kingdom of heaven; and whatsoever thou shalt bind on earth, shall be bound in heaven; and whatsoever thou shalt loose on earth, shall be loosed in heaven.
—Matthew 16:20 IV / 16:19 in other versions

Then said Jesus to them again, Peace be unto you; as my Father hath sent me, even so send I you. And when he had said this, he breathed on them, and saith unto them, Receive ye the Holy Ghost; Whosesoever sins ye remit, they are remitted unto them; and whosesoever sins ye retain, they are retained. —John 20:21-23

In the New Testament keys symbolize the rule and authority entrusted to the church by Jesus Christ, who alone holds them. They represent the power to act as Jesus did—to forgive sins, preach the gospel, and gather together God's people in community as the church. The imagery in Matthew's Gospel can be understood in at least two ways:

1. To "loose" is the divine power to forgive sins and thus to admit new converts into the church as well as restore repentant sinners to the fellowship. To "bind" is to announce God's judgment to unbelievers and sinners who are neither repentant nor contrite.

2. These two opposite verbs, to loose and bind, together express the total power entrusted to the apostles. As in the Old Testament where "good and bad" some-

times mean "everything" (see Genesis 24:54 IV / 24:50 in other versions), here both words could indicate that Jesus gave the apostles power to "do everything" in his name. And at the end of the apostolic age, the early church believed this power was transmitted to those ordained under the apostles' hands.

It is an easy thing to think of the keys of the kingdom in a somewhat mechanical way: acts or deeds that permit one to advance toward salvation, which is pictured as a perfected state. But to accept these keys in this way may overlook a depth of understanding regarding priesthood ministry in particular. This leads to the question: Which is more important, what an ordained person *does* or *is*?

An experience of Margaret Athey, about ten years before she was called to priesthood responsibility, is insightful. She had served the church in a multitude of ways and had been richly blessed as she ministered—teaching, singing, conducting choirs, and directing worship. That had given her a feeling of deep fulfillment and satisfaction.

> The possibility of priesthood for myself was dismissed quickly with the thought that I certainly had enough to do already and would not have time for more.
>
> Two or three times, unexplainable things have happened that have brought strength and enlightenment. One such incident occurred about ten years ago during a stake conference after leading the choir in singing "The Spirit of God Like a Fire Is Burning." The music had been wonderful with the organ, trumpets, and descant. We had worked hard to prepare it. I also had worked with the presider to prepare the order of worship. As I sat there with my heart still pounding from the thrill of the music, it seemed that I was caught up into a vacuum—sort of a tunnel—and I heard the voice of the Lord say, "Margaret, I want more of you."

> I didn't hesitate to answer, "My Lord, you know that I don't have more time! Why, I already go to church four nights a week and several hours on Sunday. I have a lot of responsibilities in my congregation, and I try to do them faithfully. Plus, I teach school *every* day and have a husband and three growing children who keep me busy, not to mention several professional and community things!"
>
> ...But God "spoke" to me again (I never "saw" anything and the people near me were not aware of my encounter), "Margaret, I don't want more of your time, I want more of *you*."
>
> ...I have learned that priesthood is more than officiating at the sacraments and ordinances. It means offering spiritual guidance, ministering with the power of God wherever and whenever the need arises.[2]

Priesthood Accountability

Although Section 156 has become almost a "code word" for the issue of women's ordination, that actually received little more than passing mention in the actual document: "Therefore, do not wonder that some women of the church are being called to priesthood responsibilities. This is in harmony with my will." Ultimately what may be far more important is the stress placed on purpose, preparation, and accountability of priesthood: "The power of this priesthood was placed in your midst...for the blessing and salvation of humanity." This indicates clearly that priesthood ministry should have nothing to do with position, honor, or personal advancement. Yet that apparently has happened, and now that the Temple is finally being built, it is time for it to stop. It is, then, no mere coincidence that the ministerial roles of priesthood and member are tied together with the Temple. The overarching purpose is the same: The church as the body of Christ, which is symbolized architecturally in the Temple, must reflect the servant example of Jesus Christ.

Priesthood and members alike are accountable to God through the church. Their calling as member or ordained minister is not independent of the church community; the authority they represent and the power they express arise from this servant community modeled after Christ. Perhaps now that women are being called to serve in additional ways, we can use this opportunity of newness to reinterpret the functioning of priesthood in particular. Barbara Higdon has said that her first reaction to Section 156 was a mixture of fear and rejoicing, in part because

> our movement had never come to terms theologically with the role of priesthood. We had put priesthood members on pedestals, making the unordained second-class persons. There was, it seemed to me, a great need to sort out job descriptions for the ordained and the unordained before adding to the priesthood ranks. Ordaining women, I feared, would take pressure off of our need to do that kind of analysis.
>
> As I have lived with the reality of Section 156, I have changed my position in several respects. Although painful, the turmoil in the church has provided a necessary sifting. Many people who have been negative and against any change for years have "selected" themselves out of the fellowship. The presence of some of those, although certainly not all, had held back their congregations and driven away positive people who were tired of obstruction and negativism.
>
> Furthermore, the kind of analysis and discipline I felt was needed in defining roles for ordained and unordained probably never would have taken place without Section 156. We have a long way yet to go, certainly, but we are moving closer as an institution to a better understanding of the contribution of each one than we ever would have if things had stayed the same.[3]

One central purpose of the Temple is "leadership education for priesthood and member" (Doctrine and Covenants 156:5d). That led many years ago to the establishment of Temple School. Yet some Saints, including a number of priesthood members, are uncomfortable with requiring any kind of educational competency before ordination or on a continuing basis afterward. Their reluctance, perhaps, arises from an understanding of ministerial "chosenness" that is bestowed by God directly through the Holy Spirit at the moment of ordination. This would indicate that priesthood rights and authority are independent of the community in which they find expression. However, that is directly at odds with a concept of ministry based on *service* to other persons. The call, after all, "is for workers in the cause of Zion" (Doctrine and Covenants 155:8).

The teachings of Jesus provide special emphasis to consideration of authority and power within the body of Christ. The parable of the wedding feast in Luke 14 and the story of Jesus washing his disciples' feet in John 13 emphasize humility and service as opposed to the more common human tendencies to seek position and glory.

A Prophetic People

The Restoration movement has always cherished its prophetic nature. Frequently this is understood in relation to the office of prophet. But there is a larger meaning in which the entire community is seen to be prophetic. Elbert A. Dempsey, Jr., has written,

> Divine wisdom does not consist of knowing the unknowable but of understanding the inner reality of events. Prophets are not escapists; they are activists.

> They are not otherworldly visionaries; they are the ultimate realists determined to better this world. Indeed, prophecy is God's attempt to persuade people to serve the cause of Zion. Consider some of the definitions of prophecy.
>
> - God being pastoral in our midst
> - God being relevant to our needs through a human agent
> - The divine perspective brought to bear on the affairs of life
> - The remarkable chemistry of an enlightened mind illumined by the infinite
> - A heightened insight into the inner reality of things
>
> When the pastoral resources of the church cultivate this vision of prophecy and its relationship to the cause of Zion, the members can become uniquely gifted to promote God's purposes. When the missionary tools of the church dramatize the exciting potential of a prophetic church, we can achieve a resurgence of expansion and enthusiasm. The cause of Zion can then be served with transforming power.[4]

Jacquelyn Grant has identified five key threads in the "prophetic church." These include the following: (1) the ability to discern the will of God; (2) exposing the oppressive nature of society; (3) being an agent of admonition; (4) confronting evil and not shrinking from confrontation; and (5) seeking to create a community of faith, partnership, justice, and unity.[5]

Although not expressed as such, both of these writers identify the prophetic nature of Temple ministries. The Temple, then, can serve as a symbol of our partnership with God in discerning our times as we seek to minister in the name of Jesus Christ. The discovery of our prophetic calling—our ministry as the body of Christ in a world filled with beauty and ugliness, sorrow and joy, abundance and poverty—may come in unique ways on the "holy ground" of the Temple. To be a prophetic people is not a simple thing but calls for a blending of insight and empowerment. Velma Ruch sees it this way: "This discovery, I believe, is a gift from the Restoration movement of which I am a part. From it I received a heritage of a blend of the heart and the mind, of faith and reason, of worship and education that culminated in a passion for mission, a desire to make a difference in the transformation of persons and social structures."[6]

Notes

1. Adapted from a story quoted by William R. White, *Stories for the Journey: A Sourcebook for Christian Storytellers* (Minneapolis, Minnesota: Augsburg Publishing House, 1988), 53-54.
2. Carol Anderson Anway, ed., *Extending the Call: Testimonies of Ordained Women* (Independence, Missouri: Herald Publishing House, 1989), 24-25.
3. Ibid., 126-127.
4. Elbert A. Dempsey, Jr., *The Power of the Prophetic* (Independence, Missouri: Herald Publishing House, 1988), 291-292.
5. Jacquelyn Grant, "Tasks of a Prophetic Church," *Detroit II Conference Papers* (Orbis, 1982).
6. Velma Ruch, "My Heart Was Full," *Distinguished Author Lectures, 1988-1989, Volume 1* (Independence, Missouri: Herald Publishing House, 1989), 64.

Originally published in ***Studies in the Doctrine & Covenants, Volume 3*** *(Independence, Missouri: Herald Publishing House, 1989), 30-34.*

10

Witness of the Lord Jesus Christ

Let my word be preached to the bruised and the brokenhearted as well as those who are enmeshed in sin, longing to repent and follow me. Let the truths of my gospel be proclaimed as widely and as far as the dedication of the Saints, especially through the exercise of their temporal stewardship, will allow. My Spirit is reaching out to numerous souls even now and there are many who will respond if you, my people, will bear affirmative testimony of my love and my desires for all to come unto me. Be steadfast and trust in the instructions which have been given for your guidance. I will be with you and strengthen you for the tasks that lie ahead if you will continue to be faithful and commit yourselves without reservation to the building of my kingdom.

—Doctrine and Covenants 153:9a-c

[The temple] shall also be for a strengthening of faith and preparation for witness. By its ministries an attitude of wholeness of body,

mind, and spirit as a desirable end toward which to strive will be fostered.

—Doctrine and Covenants 156:5b-c

I, the Lord, am well pleased with the progress of your preparations toward the building of my temple in the Center Place. Those who have prepared themselves by training and education to assist, whether within the body or otherwise, will be blessed according to their need insofar as they seek me and call on my name. If they will thus open themselves, then I will pour out my Spirit on all the laborers together, to the end that a shining symbol of my love and my desires for my creation may rise in beauty before the world.

— Doctrine and Covenants 157:8

Dear Saints, have courage for the task which is yours in bringing to pass the cause of Zion. Prepare yourselves through much study and earnest prayer. Then, as you go forth to witness of my love and my concern for all persons, you will know the joy which comes from devoting yourselves completely to the work of the kingdom. To this end will my Spirit be with you. Amen. —Doctrine and Covenants 156:11a-b

Joseph Sittler tells the story of a woman who attended the church where he served as interim pastor for a year. She was hooked on the "me and Jesus" movement, and she used prayer as a kind of personal lubricant to everything she wanted.

> She worked at a hospital in Chicago, and she used to tell me, "Every morning when I drive from my house to

> the hospital, I pray to Jesus that he will find me a parking spot. And you know, pastor, he always does." I kept asking myself, "What kind of God-relationship is built on this parking-space-finding Jesus that will sustain this woman in profound deprivation and tragedy? Is it enough?"
>
> One Sunday morning I said to her, "Emma, suppose there is another woman driving in the second lane on the highway taking a sick child to the hospital, and you drive right in to the parking space that Jesus found for you, and this woman who is frantic with a sick child can't find a space. How about her?"
>
> "She didn't pray hard enough," was her retort.
>
> That really stumped me. So I tried to think of how to correct her, but she was immune to argument.
>
> Well, finally I found one, and I am sinfully proud of it; I think it was a straight gift. The next time I saw her I said, "You know this speech you give me about Jesus finding you a parking space, Emma. What do you suppose Mary was praying about jogging along on that donkey on her way to Bethlehem?" Emma never mentioned the topic again. If Mary couldn't find a parking space in which to have a baby, particularly *that* baby, then there must be something wrong with the parking-space-finding Jesus.[1]

Clearly, Emma's Jesus was a sort of "Palm Sunday" and "Easter morning" Christ *without* the experiences of the intervening week—particularly the poignant heartache of Gethsemane, betrayal by a close friend, trial and public humiliation, cruel scourging by his guards, and painful death on the cross. As well, it ignores the loneliness and bewilderment of his followers during the time his lifeless body lay in the tomb. How and why could God have allowed this to happen? Perhaps Emma confidently witnessed of Jesus Christ from a narrow perspective because she accepted her understanding of Jesus as *the* understanding. Of course, she is not the only Christian who has made that mistake. In fact, that error has been repeated throughout the history of Christianity and the Restoration movement.

The Unknowable Christ

It might be good to recall an ancient Oriental saying found in both Sanskrit and the Chinese *Tao-te Ching*: "He who thinks he knows, doesn't know. He who knows that he doesn't know, knows. For in this context, to know is not to know. And not to know is to know."[2] At first, this saying seems somewhat baffling, but it actually points rather well to the mystery or unknowableness of Jesus Christ. In the end, Christ is not a doctrine that can be rationally explained nor are we talking just about a historical figure whose life and teachings are recorded in a history book. No matter how much we learn of Christ, there will always be more to learn. The descriptive titles that have been attached over the centuries—Messiah, Son of God, Son of Man, the Good Shepherd, Prince of Peace, Redeemer, Savior, Lord—expand our speculations but do not provide the complete answer.

Perhaps an important key to our understanding comes with a saying of Jesus: "I am the way, the truth, and the life; no man cometh unto the Father, but by me.... He that hath seen me hath seen the Father" (John 14:6, 9). This particular scripture has been much used in evangelism efforts, often with an understanding that the Christian—*or Restoration*—way is the *only* valid way to know God. Yet once again we are faced with the same kind of particularity that afflicted Emma and her "me and Jesus" thinking. But if we accept the idea that "not to know is to know," then we must allow ourselves to be open to other interpretations such as this:

> God comes to us in Jesus who is the way. We are like people who have fallen into a pit and in that fall have been injured. Our legs and our arms are broken. For anyone to lower a ladder into the pit and say, "This is the only way out, climb it," only adds to our desperation. But if the ladder is lowered not for us to climb out, but for one to climb down and lift our broken body into his arms, carrying us upwards and to safety—that is good news indeed![3]

When Jesus says he is "the way," is he saying his private path to God is the only way anyone can ever hope to get to heaven or experience salvation? Is he saying that he alone holds the secret formula to unlock the mysteries and if we do all the right things and affirm all the *right* beliefs, those secrets will be shared with us? No. As A. M. Watts has written,

> Jesus' words are more like those of a scientist describing gravity. When Jesus says "no one comes to the Father but by me," he is stating that ultimately no one comes to God except through God, no one comes to God's glory except through God's humility and no one comes to the self-giving Father except through the self-giving Son....
>
> To affirm that God was in Christ reconciling the world to Godself is not ground for believing that people of other religious traditions are all wrong. To affirm such an arrogant principle is not the way to affirm Christ. Indeed, if Christ is God in God's self-giving to humanity, there can be no ground for Christian arrogance.[4]

There is no room for arrogance within the Restoration church that offers the Temple as a witness of Jesus Christ and "shining symbol of [God's] love." Prophetic direction given in 1988 specifically admonishes the church that its members should "not be lifted up in pride as you contemplate the work of building, neither think to raise up my temple in vanity" so the resources offered sacrificially by Temple builders can be "offered joyfully but humbly to a world in need" (Doctrine and Covenants 157:9). The Temple shall stand, as well, not so much as evidence of "what we know" as "who we seek"; it will be less a case of "Jesus dwells here" than "God in Christ *is*." And the best way to "discover Christ" is to be like Jesus—healer, reconciler, and servant.

Jesus as Reconciler

Kisuke Sekine, through his family heritage of Buddhism and his own calling as an apostle of the Lord Jesus Christ, offers the church a unique perspective in regard to Jesus as reconciler.

> Hands, depending on how we wish to use them, can become powerful weapons of destruction, or a means to attain inner peace and to heal wounded souls and broken hearts through reconciliation with self and with others....
>
> [In] some parts of my cultural world, people greet each other by folding their hands in front—*Sawadee* or *Namaste*. What is the meaning, the significance, of folded hands?
>
> We fold our hands so the joy of the right hand can be shared with the left, thus multiplying our joy. We fold our hands so the burdens of the left can be shared with the right, thus the burdens can be lightened. We fold our hands so the determination of the right can be supported by the left, thus the determination can be strengthened.
>
> Hands can express innermost feelings that are often indescribable in words. They can impart power beyond human comprehension, often performing miracles of healing physical, mental, and spiritual disturbances, restoring harmony and peace in the life of both the extender and recipient.
>
> Hands are used by performing artists in dance, play, music, martial arts; by scientists in exploring the "un-

knowns" yet to be revealed; by those in ministry to express and convey God's love and concern for his creation. Hands, so uniquely given us, are used to express appreciation of the beauty of creation, as well as to restore its balance and reconcile its chaos to cosmos. This enables us to see beyond the curtain of mystery the true meaning and purpose of life in God's wondrous creation.[5]

A Two-way Street

The Temple will rise as a beacon that calls humankind to join hands and share Christ. This will mean a two-way street for the church. First, the Temple will provide a means of empowerment for the Saints so they will be prepared to go into the world as servants ready to bear the burdens of sin in the stead of Christ. A good deal of this will come through the channel of Temple School, for there is much more to "burden bearing" than mere willingness—it will take education, training, and practice. Second, the Temple will attract people from all over the world to share their understandings of Divinity with the Restoration church. As such, church members need to be open to more truth and new pathways of knowledge. Such a two-way street as this probably will require a reevaluation of the church's evangelism efforts.

Of course, the Reorganized Church of Jesus Christ of Latter Day Saints is not alone in its need to reinterpret the way it shares the gospel of Christ. Samuel L. Dunn, writing in *The Futurist* magazine, sees the twenty-first century as a time of challenge and change for Christianity in Western Europe and North America. Theological, political, demographic, and economic developments will force the church in these countries to, among other things he says, take a backseat in the management of world evangelization. "The church in these countries will find, to a large extent, its agenda set by others."[6]

Dunn foresees that by the year 2025 Christians in first-world countries (Western Europe and North America primarily) will comprise no more than one-fourth of all the world Christians. The majority of believers in Christ will live in the southern hemisphere—South America, Africa, and the Indian subcontinent in particular—and more will speak Spanish than any other language. But what is even more significant than that is his suggestion that by 2025 local administrative control of almost all church and missionary programs should be in the hands of local officials.

> Most church organizations in second- and third-world countries will be endogenized, maintaining only theological and fraternal ties with founding churches in the first world. The church in the first world will continue to provide financial support, technical assistance, and influence, but such assistance will be received at the invitation of and under the direction of local leaders.[7]

Christianity, of course, has been a missionary religion ever since Jesus issued the Great Commission to go into all the world and make disciples of all nations. Because Christianity has been centered in Europe and North America, that is where most missionaries have originated. In the last five centuries, Dunn states, four levels of relationship have existed between the branch of the church sending missionaries and the receiving church:

1. ***Paternalism:*** missionaries maintained total control because they viewed the target populations as culturally deprived and intellectually inferior.

2. ***Partnership:*** although the target populations were accepted as individuals with significant cultures and as

intellectual equals, *de facto* control remained with the sending church because that's where the money came from.

3. ***Indigenization:*** administration is given to local church officials although missionaries from the sending church offer technical assistance, specialized ministries, and provide financial support, and their way of doing things is still the preferred style.

4. ***Endogenization:*** the church is fully under local control, elements of local culture are used in Christian worship, and church governance is carried on in a manner normal to that culture; representatives of the sending church are present *only* by invitation of local officials; the national church is a full and equal partner with the sending church.

An Endogenized RLDS Church

The Independence Temple *can* be a highly useful tool and symbol as the RLDS Church engages in endogenization. Of course, that is not inevitable, for it will be very easy to see the Temple as belonging just to North American culture. Unless the church actively promotes it in relation to endogenization, that is all the Temple will stand for as far as people outside the affluent classes of the English-speaking world are concerned. That the Temple as an architectural symbol of Christ *is there* in the center of our faith community offering a universal appeal may be of great significance in and of itself. The story of "The Rabbi's Gift" by Francis Dorff can help us understand this kind of role for the Temple. An adaptation of that story follows:

Once there was a famous monastery that had fallen on difficult times. Where once its buildings had been filled with young monks and its chapel echoed with the singing of the chant, now it was deserted. No one came any longer to find spiritual nourishment, and a mere handful of aging monks shuffled through the cloisters to praise God with heavy hearts.

Not far from the monastery, on the edge of a nearby forest, an old rabbi had built a small hut. From time to time he would come to fast and pray. Nobody ever spoke to him, but whenever he appeared, the word would be passed from monk to monk, "The rabbi walks in the woods." For as long as the rabbi was there, the monks would feel sustained by his prayerful presence.

One day the abbot decided to visit the rabbi and open his heavy heart to him. So, after the morning Eucharist, he set out through the woods. While standing in the doorway of the hut, the rabbi saw the abbot coming and stretched out his arms in welcome. It was almost as though he had been waiting for some time, and the two embraced like long-lost brothers.

After the two had stood awhile smiling in the doorway, the rabbi motioned the abbot to enter. In the center of the sparsely furnished room was a table with the scriptures open on it. They sat for a moment in the presence of "the Book," then the rabbi began to cry. The old abbot could not contain himself either. For the first time in his life, he cried his heart out. The two men sat there like lost children and filled the hut with their sobs.

After a long time, the rabbi lifted his head and said, "You and your brothers are serving God with heavy hearts. You have come to ask a teaching of me. I will give it to you, but you can only repeat it once. After that, no one must ever say it aloud again."

The rabbi looked right at the abbot's eyes and said, "The Messiah is among you." All was silent for a few minutes, then he added, "Now you must go."

The abbot left without a word and without looking back. The next morning he called his monks together. He told them he had received a teaching from "the rabbi who walks in the woods" and that this teaching was never to be spoken aloud again. After looking at each of his brothers he said, "The rabbi said that one of us is the Messiah."

The monks were startled. "What could it mean?" they asked themselves. "Is Brother Matthew the Messiah? Or Father Thomas? Or Brother John? Am I the Messiah?" They were all deeply puzzled, but no one ever mentioned it again.

As time went by, the monks began to treat one another with a special reverence. There was a gentle, wholehearted, human quality about them now that was hard to describe but easy to notice. They lived with one another as men who had finally found something, and they lived with one another as men who were always looking for something. Visitors to the monastery were deeply moved by the life of these monks, and before long people were coming from far and wide to be nourished by the prayer life of the monks. Young men began asking once again to become part of the community.

In those days, the rabbi no longer walked in the woods. His hut had fallen into ruins. But somehow or other, the old monks who had taken his teaching to heart still felt sustained by his prayerful presence.

Many Things to Many People

The Temple is sure to become many things to many people. As symbol, facilitator, sacred space, and advocate for peace, its role in the twenty-first-century church is just beginning to be explored. Certainly the Temple—as a concept and as an actual structure—has its detractors. There are those who believe the $75 million cost for building and endowing it could be better spent elsewhere. Some may be disappointed that the Independence Temple will not recreate previous temples in Jerusalem, Kirtland, Nauvoo, or the one at first envisaged for Independence, or the several later proposed. Others may object to the absence of millennial or apocalyptic characteristics. Indeed, this may even prompt us to seek to redefine the term "Latter Day Saints." Sadly, some Saints will disregard the Temple simply because "it's on the wrong side of the street," thereby missing entirely its meaning and purpose.

But there will also be many who will respond to the call of Christ to "follow." After all, this Temple *belongs* to Christ and will stand as a beacon along Christ's "way." The spiritual journeys that believers will take to come to the Temple and the directions it will send them back into the world as sacrificial servants, reconcilers, healers, and peacemakers will be as varied as the cultures they represent. The building of the Temple, in this sense, may well represent the beginning of the most exciting, stimulating, and enriching period in church history as we continually rediscover Jesus Christ.

Notes

1. Joseph Sittler, *Gravity & Grace: Reflections and Provocations* (Minneapolis: Augsburg Publishing House, 1986), 39-40. Used with permission.
2. Quoted in Joseph Campbell, *The Power of Myth* (New York: Doubleday, 1988), 55.
3. From a sermon by Henk Booy quoted in A.M. Watts, "Christian Claims in a Pluralistic Society," *The Christian Century* Vol. 106, No. 7 (March 1, 1989): 223. Copyright 1989 Christian Century Foundation. Reprinted by permission from the March 1, 1989, issue of *The Christian Century*.
4. Ibid.
5. Kisuke Sekine, "The Essence of Reconciliation," *Saints Herald* Vol. 135, No. 7 (July 1988): 7-8.
6. Samuel L. Dunn, "Christianity's Future: The First-World Church Takes a Back Seat," *The Futurist* (March-April 1989): 34. Used with permission.
7. Ibid, 35-36.
8. Adapted from a story quoted by William R. White, *Stories for the Journey: A Sourcebook for Christian Storytellers* (Minneapolis, Minnesota: Augsburg Publishing House, 1988), 108- 110.

Epilogue

A little more than twenty years ago, during my freshman year at Graceland College, doctors first diagnosed a chronic disease of my digestive system. They called it regional enteritis, or more simply ileitis. I have since come to know it as Crohn's disease. Nobody told me then that diagnosis would profoundly change my life. I probably wouldn't have believed them even if they had. That first episode of Crohn's was a shock, but after successful treatment with drug therapy, my life resumed without too many changes.

I went on to pursue a career as a journalist, and I learned to seek the five W's: who, what, where, when, and why. Somewhere along the way a seasoned newspaper editor shortened that list for me down to the basics: What? and So What? Trying to answer those two questions has since become practically second-nature. It is an approach that has served me well, whether in my jobs, personal relationships, church responsibilities, or subsequent episodes of Crohn's.

Yes, the Crohn's has returned a few times. I've lost track of the number of tubes and scopes that have been stuck in my mouth, nose, and rectum. Even strawberry-flavored barium solutions still retain an unpleasant taste. A few years back a surgeon removed lengthy portions of my small intestine, and I've gotten used to seeing a much thinner person in the bathroom mirror every morning. Crohn's is a curious disease in that nobody dies from it. But it can wear down the body's immune system, leaving one more susceptible to viruses, germs, and infections. I've adapted slowly by changing my life-style. Wholeness and health have a much different meaning for me today as I've learned the best way to respond to what my body is telling me.

It is a curious fact that I've learned more from my own body about Crohn's than from all the doctors, nurses, and technicians. Most of them, I've found, don't quite know what to do with a disease that has no known cause or cure. All they can do with this chronic condition is more or less pretend it's not there so they can treat the symptoms with standard acute-care procedures. And they *do* succeed with that. But they fail in the fight against Crohn's, and that troubles them. No matter what they do, they cannot make me as healthy as they are. It is almost an affront to modern medicine. Perhaps some even pity me because of my physical shortcomings.

Especially those without a Christian faith cannot fathom the paradox of how my brokenness has led me toward finding a different kind of strength, the kind offered by the Great Physician. The Gospels of Matthew, Mark, and Luke all record Jesus' words that the well have no need of a physician, only the sick, which is the reason for his mission and ministry. This profound Christian metaphor is not too hard to understand. Yet who of us does not need the ministry of Christ, and what can that tell us about our own health and well-being, both physical and spiritual? Wherever I look in the church, I find Saints ready to heal the sick and sinful, yet some haven't a clue that they, themselves, are less than whole and healthy.

When I see that a central purpose of the Temple is related to the wholeness of body, mind, and spirit, Temple ministry takes on a special meaning for me. It makes me wonder how those without any experience with chronic illnesses view the healing ministry of the

Temple. Are we guaranteeing failure when we see our ministry as making sick people "healthy like we are" because we have denied our own brokenness? In other words, can Temple ministry offered by a people denying the reality of their own condition bring hope and deliverance to a sin-sick world? So what will it matter that the Temple will stand in the center of our faith community?

A decade or two from now, will the church carry on in much the same way as it does today, only with a pretty building in which tours and occasional worship services are offered? If I were to say that the reality of the Temple in our midst will profoundly alter the church from this moment onward, *so what*? In these essays I've written of transforming the church, of becoming the body of Christ in sacrificial service to the world. Will the Temple really matter?

I'm reminded of a comment made by theologian H. Richard Niebuhr a few years ago. He worried that making Christianity merely relevant might result in a pseudo-gospel in which a "God without wrath brought people without sin into a kingdom without judgment through the ministrations of a Christ without a cross." Will the members of the Reorganized Church of Jesus Christ of Latter Day Saints be up to taking the tough road by being a Good Friday as well as an Easter people? Can we accept our brokenness, suffering, sacrifice, and limitations so divine grace can come through us to others?

Life goes on, regardless. On this gray, early winter day just after Thanksgiving 1990, I am amazed at how a parking lot has been transformed in the short time since the Temple groundbreaking on April 6. Steel girders are being hoisted in place for the two-story office portion of the Temple complex; the 200-foot-tall shoring tower stands bleakly, waiting for erection of the sanctuary's steel spiral. This is an exciting time for the church. But eventually people will stand on the same spot I do and see a completed building, a unique architectural wonder and accepted fact of life in Independence, Missouri. *So what?* By then, will the Temple have lived up to our hopes and dreams, or will future Saints shake their heads in dismay at the colossal waste of it all?

Of course, the Temple may have no effect on some in the church. They will recognize no change, and the building may simply reinforce what they see as the strengths of a healthy religious institution. I have denied the presence of Crohn's many times in my life, yet eventually I accepted a new reality. I am neither self-sufficient nor able to do all I want to do. In other words, I need other people—to work with them, among them, and for them. In doing so I've discovered how to receive strength and how to give it.

Several themes run throughout the essays in this book: mutual empowerment, prophetic community, sacrificial service, the people of God, pursuit of peace, grace, equality, and honesty. Perhaps they are difficult or even foreign concepts to some church members today. After all, we are used to rigid hierarchies where a few men make decisions on behalf of everyone else. We are wary of looking too closely at our own history, perhaps fearful of discovering that our familiar, cherished stories make better faith statements than honest, historical reflection. Or maybe we find the task of seeking a fresh word of God far more difficult than relying on existing scriptures. Sometimes, in the absence of relevant light and truth, it *is* easier to wait on our prophet to essentially decide for us.

These are hard realities to ponder, and it is natural not to want to deal with them. I, too, have often preferred to sing, "All is well, all is well." But I know I should not pretend it were so. The Temple is the most exciting, most wonderful, and riskiest enterprise in which the church has ever engaged. Perhaps the way we should go about it is something like living with a chronic illness, and I think the church can learn much from that approach. All the words in these and other essays will be just so many good intentions unless we first accept our own brokenness and our need for Christ, the Great Physician. Otherwise, our efforts will be as futile as the doctors who have tried to heal my Crohn's by treating the symptoms. At times I may appear as physically healthy as those without this chronic condition, but it is really just a facade. What is inside me eventually finds outward expression. I don't want the Temple to be a facade, a pretty symbol hiding our denials and insecurities.

I've come full circle, and probably I'm no closer to answering the "So What?" questions now than in the beginning. That may just highlight another connection between chronic illness and the Temple: There are no final, absolute answers. Life will go on, regardless. Yet I cannot speak to future generations who will know and use the Temple intimately. This book was not written primarily for them anyway. It was written for *our* journey in which Christ goes with us into the world. With every new encounter we—who dare to speak of ourselves as the body of Christ—will keep on asking "What?" and "So What?" and take one more step toward the peaceful reign of God on earth.